THE
KEYS
TO
UNLOCKING
GOD'S
WEALTH

TIME FOR CHANGE.
TIME FOR A NEW MINDSET!

Liam McNamara

The Keys To Unlocking God's Wealth
Copyright © 2018 Liam McNamara
ISBN: 978-1-9997955-2-8

All rights reserved.
No part of this publication may be reproduced, stored in a retrieval system, or transmitted in any form or by any means, electronic, mechanical, photocopying or otherwise, without prior written consent of the publisher except as provided by under United Kingdom copyright law. Short extracts may be used for review purposes with credits given.

All Scriptures quoted are taken from New King James Version, except where stated. Scripture taken from the New King James Version®. Copyright © 1982 by Thomas Nelson. Used by permission. All rights reserved.

Scripture quotations from The Authorized (King James) Version. Rights in the Authorized Version in the United Kingdom are vested in the Crown. Reproduced by permission of the Crown's patentee, Cambridge University Press.

THE HOLY BIBLE, NEW INTERNATIONAL VERSION®, NIV® Copyright © 1973, 1978, 1984, 2011 by Biblica, Inc.® Used by permission. All rights reserved worldwide.

Scripture taken from The Message. Copyright © 1993, 1994, 1995, 1996, 2000, 2001, 2002. Used by permission of NavPress Publishing Group.

Scripture quotations marked (TLB) are taken from The Living Bible copyright © 1971. Used by permission of Tyndale House Publishers, Inc., Carol Stream, Illinois 60188. All rights reserved.

Published by
Maurice Wylie Media
Bethel Media House, Tobermore
Northern Ireland
BT45 5SJ (UK)

Publishers' statement: Throughout this book the love for our God is such that whenever we refer to Him we honour with Capitals. On the other hand, when referring to the devil, we refuse to acknowledge him with any honour to the point of violating grammatical rule and withholding capitalisation.

For more information visit
www.MauriceWylieMedia.com

DISCLAIMER:
All counsel should be taken through a professional. Neither the publisher nor the author shall be liable for any other loss, including but not limited to special, incidental, or consequential, or other damages.

CONTENTS

CHAPTER ONE: **Setting the scene...**   9
        Power for living   14

CHAPTER TWO: **Do we really understand money?...**   18
        Finding God's cattle   20
        Tax reconciliation   22
        The Lord has a plan   26
        Release from debt   29

CHAPTER THREE: **The money world...**   33
        The origin of money   34
        Inflation   37
        Recession or wealth transfer?   38

CHAPTER FOUR: **Seeing the money world as a Christian...**   41
        The spiritual battlefield   44
        God wants us to prosper   47

CHAPTER FIVE: **The bondage of debt...**	49
Not a formula	57
Dealing with fear	58
CHAPTER SIX: **Wealth vs poverty...**	62
CHAPTER SEVEN: **Power to get wealth...**	73
God's pattern	76
Finding wealth	80
CHAPTER EIGHT: **The purpose of wealth...**	83
CHAPTER NINE: **Stewardship...**	87
Lessons on stewardship	90
Stewardship of money	94
CHAPTER TEN: **Giving and receiving...**	99
Sowing a seed	103
CHAPTER ELEVEN: **Praying for finances...**	105
CHAPTER TWELVE: **Learning about money...**	112
Final thoughts	114
Declaration	116

DEDICATION

I am so grateful to my wife Mary who has encouraged me over such a long time, to write this book. Together, we have both come to see first-hand, the scarcity and lack of money in the lives of our Christian brothers and sisters and the churches to which they belong. Through our engagement with churches throughout the country and outreach projects which we have helped launch, we have witnessed the cruelty and hardship in what God's people goes through due to in many instances the lack of money.

While witnessing all this, our Lord has brought us on a journey in our personal and business life, to experience breakthrough as set out in His Word. We are passionate in our desire to share this experience.

Scripture tells us to go and make disciples. A disciple is a mature follower of Jesus, walking in fellowship with Him, being led by the Holy Spirit. Many churches are busy making converts and not disciples. This means that there are lots of spiritual babies who have not grown. I believe these babies become a playground for satan and because, as babies, they do not understand what is happening, many will fall away.

One of the greatest tools used by satan to ensure that many Christians remain as babies is, he deceives us about money. What we need is, a 'God understanding' of money. If we do not understand God's ways relating to money, then instead of us having control of money, money will control us, spiraling its victims into debt, bankruptcy and even for some, premature death.

As Christians we are called to possess the land but have you ever asked what is the most common giant within the Church? The answer is 'debt!' Throughout Scripture we can read many times of how God's people were stripped, some stripped naked and left for dead… This is a form of bankruptcy. But God has given us keys to be wise to the thief and if we use His keys, the thief cannot steal. Remember Scripture states…

'For I know the plans I have for you, declares the Lord, plans to prosper you and not to harm you, plans to give you hope and a future.' Jeremiah 29:11

I pray that you will find encouragement, wisdom and breakthrough reading this book, to grow to the fullness of who God planned for you to be and through this, to be able to share with others, the fullness and truth of God's Word.

Liam

FOREWORD

Liam McNamara is one of the most inspiring people I have ever met. Over the years that I have known him personally, I have witnessed first-hand the impact that his tender compassion towards people has yielded in their lives. With a dogged determination that has been borne out from his personal journey; Liam is passionate about people and passionate about making a difference in their lives.

In this book we discover something about its author and something about ourselves, in engaging with one of the most global and universal struggles that we all have, to some degree or other, our relationship with money. In this engagement, we also discover something about the reality of the person who is God.

Sharing candidly and vulnerably, Liam combines his own life lessons forged from the mistakes, pain and turmoil of his past with his many years of professionally recognised business acumen. Liam offers us, as readers, help in our understanding about our relationship to money, as well as offering us hope that God is more involved in our story and in our journey than we might realise.

This book is an open account of one man's lifelong learning and his desire to gift that learning to those who need it. Perhaps in order to spare us similar fate, or at least to give us faith that our story, no matter how good or how bad - is not finished. No matter where we are in our personal struggles, battles and tensions brought on by money... We can become its master and not its servant.

It is my great pleasure to introduce this simple but powerful piece of literature to the world and to encourage you to jump in with an open heart. I am sure that if you do, not only will you learn something, but you may get more out of it than you now realise.

We all need money... Therefore we all need a little help sometimes with our relationship with money... Often we need hope when it comes to the challenges that money or the lack thereof uniquely brings into our lives.

Hope this blesses you as much as it did me.

Jamie Corcoran

Lead Pastor, Lighthouse Community Church, Navan, Ireland.

CHAPTER ONE

Setting the scene...

I have had a long and tempestuous relationship with money for 38 years of which, sometimes I would win and sometimes I wouldn't. I have allowed money to beat me, even to the extent that I lost my home and everything I had; but I will go into that later.

As a child I believed in God, but in my late teens I felt I could not comply with the standards that seemed to be demanded of me, so I gave up on my faith. Wealth became my god as I focused my attention on accumulating money and becoming independent through this, believing that if one was wealthy, one has everything, and as such I would be fulfilled.

In my family, I was the eldest, I had a brother and a sister and we lived at home with my mother and my father. We lived in my father's childhood home farm in Limerick, it was a small, thatched house with only three rooms. The kitchen, living room and one bedroom. The conditions were dire so my father worked hard to make things better for us by establishing his own business.

He had built up a successful dairy herd and had a contracting machinery business. He was well known throughout the local area. As his business flourished, it created an environment in which I learned that life can be good with money.

Things were improving for our family, however, when my father was 55-years-old, he developed a heart condition and within a four-week period I watched my family's wealth *literally* go out our front gate.

Cows had to be sold, machinery was sold, it was all taken away. My mother was trying to hold it all together but it wasn't working, we were only kids and couldn't help her.

This had a significant impact on my life at this early age, it put a steely determination into me that I was going to get back my father's money. I didn't know how but I knew one day, I would do it. I believed that reclaiming this money was all that mattered in life, and that became my driving factor. It also taught me a huge life lesson about the fragility of money. I saw how we were so dependent on it, yet it was fragile and could be lost at any time.

It was shortly after my father lost his business that I turned against God. I was 17-years-old at the time and I had decided to make my own way in life. Most of the farm was cleared out by this stage but there were still a few cows in the yard, so I had to get up early to milk them before school. My mother and I had also just set up a vegetable business to try and generate some income, so I had to see to that before I left too. I had a lot of weight on my shoulders as a young boy.

One day I was on my way to school that was just outside Limerick riding my bicycle and suddenly this rage overcame me. I pulled my bike over to a gate, jumped off my bike in a fit of anger and I roared at God. I didn't care who could hear me as I punched the air and yelled; "I've had enough of You!"

This was very out of character for me as I had a strong Christian upbringing, very Catholic. My mother was very religious, we had the rosary every night and attended mass and I was taught by the Jesuits. With all the loss that we had suffered at the farm and with my father's deterioration, I was just exasperated.

That day marked the beginning of my journey alone, I was determined I could do it by myself and off I rode. I went into class that day and started planning how I would become successful in my own strength.

I loved sport and it was my success in sports that established me among my peers. I played hurling and rugby and played for my province, Munster, at school level.

When I finished my leaving cert, I couldn't afford to go to university but I won a scholarship to go to an agricultural college. I attended there for a year and a half and they then provided me with a scholarship to go to university.

I thought this was my way to really make it in the world, so I worked really hard and in 1973 I graduated and got a job with one of the big dairy product manufacturing companies. I thought I had made it! But my pursuit of money made me very selfish, self-centred and I had little respect for others in the process. This affected every area of my life as my selfishness consumed me; I did not care about the effect of my actions on others as long as *I* got what *I* wanted.

I set up my first business in 1980, building it to a turnover of €3m (€9m approx. in 2018) before selling it in 1983 for €950k (€3m in 2018) to a large Irish company. That was a lot of money at that time for a 28-year-old.

I became marketing director of that company as part of the deal with a big salary, high profile and many other benefits. This satisfied my ambition, but only for a while. I decided to leave after two and a half years and in 1986, I set up another company in partnership with a very large multinational, this partnership led company was much bigger than the one of my own I had sold. I invested every penny I had and could borrow, including re-mortgaging my dream home. I gave land that I owned and also land that my mother owned as security to the banks. I was very confident in my own abilities.

I ran this business successfully for two years until in May 1988, I found I could no longer find raw materials at a competitive price which forced me to put the business into liquidation. This was a devastating blow to me as I was used to success. I was now a high-achiever so I found it very hard to accept that it had all gone wrong.

Going into liquidation left me with debts of several million to the banks, with no income, unemployable due to the debts.

Arising from this disaster, I began to come face to face with myself. The disaster I caused was right before my eyes. I was always able to manoeuvre my way out of tricky situations. This one, however, was clearly much bigger than me.

Most people in the food industry knew what had happened and saw me as a failure, my name was now being rolled around in the mud of gossip. I knew I was going to lose our house as the mortgage on it was so big. Being married with three children aged 9, 12 and 14 that I loved dearly; I struggled to come to terms with telling them, the life they were accustomed to is now over! In a nutshell, I was completely washed up and washed out!

Just as I had, when I was a child; I began again to see how fickle and fragile wealth and money is in life and how much hope, trust, dependency and confidence I had placed on money. It was clear to me; my god of wealth had let me down.

How foolish I was for all those years. I had hurt many people on my journey of selfishness and had let them down through my pride and arrogance while I was chasing shadows. To be successful and wealthy, were heartfelt desires I carried since childhood.

However, looking back, even though I gained the success I craved, I cannot remember a moment during the good times when I really felt content and fulfilled.

All my success brought me was a desire to risk for more, even though what I had gained was great and plenty. I found it made me greedier and, through arrogance, I believed that I could achieve whatever I decided to pursue. I realised that this is what happens when you make money your god.

One of the hardest parts of my demise was when the bank took the land from my mother because of my debts. My brother and sister believed I had lost their inheritance yet my mother was more worried about me through this difficult time. It was an awful moment when I realised the bank was going to strip her of all her land, it really affected me badly. The shame I felt was overwhelming.

 ***Be determined not to be driven by flesh***

DRIVEN BY FLESH	LED BY THE SPIRIT
• You will not enjoy the journey	• Joy will be your portion each day
• Casualties will be on your left and right	• Where mistakes are done you'll seek to fix
• You're not answerable to anyone	• Wise people will be connected to you
• Accomplishments are only for a moment	• Each accomplishment is celebrated
• Soul misery	• Soul is at peace
• Storm driven	• Divine appointments

Power for living...

When I was in the middle of despair and hopelessness, I was given a book by Arthur S DeMoss called *Power for Living*. Within its pages was a story very similar to mine and the author asked the question; 'Who is Lord of your life?' Without hesitation I immediately answered: "I am!"

As soon as I said this to myself, I immediately became aware that if this was so then there are two Lords – ME *and* God.

I always believed there was a God who was supreme and who I would have to face one day, which for me, was a very long time away.

The message that was in the book that I was reading was, if I would surrender to God's Lordship, He would take care of me and my family and make everything alright.

We need to ask, "Who is sitting on the throne of our heart? Jesus or Me?

We need to get off the throne and let the Lord sit on it!

The second message in the book was that if I could be good enough to make it to heaven through my own efforts, then Jesus did not need to do what He did for me or you.

Truly I was blown away with revelation and annoyed that despite all my religious education as a child, nobody had told me this.

Even though I had made a conscious decision to reject Him earlier in life, it was with being on this journey in Him that I have witnessed what an amazing, faithful, long-suffering, patient God we serve, especially in that He would seek my attention, so He could rescue me from the pit I had fallen into.

I immediately went on my knees and surrendered my life to Jesus, determined to walk under His Lordship from then on, no matter the cost for my flesh and my ways.

Since I came to know Him, He has revealed so much to me during this time, especially regarding what I *thought* I knew about money. He has taught me a true 'understanding of money' and when you have the understanding then...*'you shall know the truth, and the truth shall make you free!'* John 8:32

Knowing about something and understanding something are two different levels of awareness. I knew about money, but it wasn't until God taught me how to understand it, that I started to be free. Remember it's the truth that you know/ understand that sets you FREE!

Through all these years I have witnessed and experienced how God took me from where I was when I met Him, to where I am today. I will share testimonies in this book of how He delivered me from my circumstances. The centrepiece of most of the testimonies relates to money.

One of the questions I often asked the Lord for many years, is why He took me from all that I knew, which was the food industry, into a completely different sector – finance, otherwise known as money. It was only in 2007 that he began to show me His purpose in this, and this is part of the reason why I have written this book.

Since becoming involved in finance through accountancy, tax and financial services, the Lord has given me insight, through developing a Scriptural understanding of *money* and all its components. The Lord has blessed me with a live experience and engagement with those who manage most of the world's money.

In the past 10 years I have had first-hand experience of the effect and control that money has in people's lives, whether they are Christian or not. This experience has been through engagement with clients who seek my advice on the challenges they are facing with money. In almost all cases I have either been in, or am currently going through these challenges myself. I see the devastation that debt is causing to families, causing hopelessness and despair and in some cases, even suicide.

Jesus told His disciples, 'Gather the pieces that are left over. Let nothing be wasted.' (John 6:12) Nothing is ever wasted in God. Learn from your mistakes in life and business, if need be, place boundaries for overspending, learn to budget, learn to never look down on a small opportunity. Even a small seed can lead into a great harvest!

Unfortunately, I have seen first-hand how churches and ministries throughout Ireland and further afield are paralysed by lack of money. The great commission of the Church is to reach the lost. In most cases, churches simply don't have the resources to do so.

God's army is paralysed by debt and unable to function in the calling that the Lord has placed on their lives.

Imagine a country sending their troops with bows and arrows to fight in this day of modern warfare. They would be wiped out, not because they would be unwilling to fight but because they don't have the resources needed to equip themselves and to take the fight to the enemy. I firmly believe this is the strategy of satan who is using money as a controlling tool for his end-time purpose before Jesus returns.

I want to share what the Lord has taught me regarding the strategies of satan and how to overcome his plans and schemes in the hope that those who will read this book will come to realise what is going on in the spiritual realm. We need to have victory over the devil's plans and schemes in order that the fullness of God's promises would manifest in our lives, enabling us to live in victory and to be available to the Lord to help Him fulfil his end-time purpose, which is to bring all those He has called into His kingdom, so that He can return.

The battles will be lost in the areas that we don't understand. The devil's sole purpose is to... 'Steal, kill and to destroy.' (John 10:10) The devil wants to steal from you and kill and destroy you. One of the areas he wins in is the area of our knowledge/ understanding of that which we lack in. Hosea 4:6; 'My people are destroyed for the lack of knowledge.'

CHAPTER TWO

Do we really understand money?

When my collapse came, the focus of my problems was money. How was I going to survive and provide for my children? I had surrendered to Jesus, but in surrendering to Jesus and then 'knowing Him,' that's a whole new level of understanding. It's like when two people become married, they can say they know each other, but its only after marriage and being together for some time that we *really* get to know each other. She has bad habits, he has bad habits but praise God, Jesus has no bad habits!

It was then I had to learn quickly that it is only in His ways that He becomes my provider and I must learn to become disciplined by following His way. As the Bible teaches us in Philippians 4:19; *'And my God shall supply all your need according to His riches in glory by Christ Jesus.'* As I read this Scripture, I realised my problem had been my understanding of money. I saw that if I didn't understand the law of money then instead of it being a tool to bless me, it actually becomes a curse to me!

This was a challenge as I had to learn to stop striving and to trust Him. I did strive at the beginning but found that most of the time I made matters worse and suffered a lot of rejection trying to get work. It was very difficult for me learning how to surrender, however, my brokenness at the time helped me develop my character to be more like Him.

I came to a place where I went before the Lord in prayer and promised that whatever He showed me to do in any day, I would do so diligently, but if He did not show me anything to do then I would sit with Him and read His Word.

This started me on my journey to freedom as He began to teach me to *walk by faith*. It also brought many challenges from those who were close to me, who would challenge me for acting irresponsibly. Over time the Lord proved Himself faithful and those friends saw the evidence of the Lord's promises manifest in my life.

One of the names of God is Jehovah Jireh, which means God our Provider. He wants to provide for us by giving us opportunities, to change our thinking, etc. We need to learn that He is the Supreme Provider and not to depend on ourselves. When we do depend on ourselves only, we will not reach the potential He has for us.

Like most of the keys, it will not come easily to many of us. The reason it is not easy for us is that we've been programmed from birth, to think and do things a certain way. For many of us we've had a puppy at some point of our life. Remember how you would have filled the bowl with food and called the puppy. The puppy ran in and turned to whatever area you would have had the bowl. Every time that call went out for food, the puppy ran in and turned to the same area the bowl was in. But change the bowl's location and watch what happens? The puppy will run in and turn the same direction as before, only to find out that the bowl is missing. Then it starts sniffing around the area, confused because the location of the bowl has been changed.

When we hear prosperity, finances, budgets, money etc. Those words make our minds run to the same location as before. If we run to the same location as before, our results will be the same. However, if we take time to reflect, that perhaps our minds need to move to a new location of thinking, then we will quickly realise that the One who wants to be our Supreme Provider is God Himself.

Finding God's cattle...

As I shared with you, I was raised on a farm, so cattle was something I knew about, but what I didn't know at that time was that God has cattle!

Scripture states, *'For every beast of the forest is Mine, And the cattle on the thousand hills!'* Psalm 50:10

Did you read that? God has cattle, we just need to know how to find them!

During this time, my home circumstances were getting poor, I remember one Friday evening in particular, we had no food and no money to buy food. It was about 4pm and my wife turned on me because of the situation we were in, and she asked me; "Where is your God now?"

I was not able to answer her but I knew that my Lord had said to me; "Do not worry." I had previously been reading in His Word the following passage which I was trying to apply to my life; *'Therefore I say to you, do not worry about your life, what you will eat or what you will drink; nor about your body, what you will put on. Is not life more than food and the body more than clothing? Look at the birds of the air, for they neither sow nor reap nor gather into barns; yet your heavenly Father feeds them. Are you not of more value than they? Which of you by worrying can add one cubit to his stature? So why do you worry about clothing? Consider the lilies of the field, how they grow: they neither toil nor spin; and yet I say to you that even Solomon in all his glory was not arrayed like one of these. Now if God so clothes the grass of the field, which today is, and tomorrow is thrown into the oven, will He not much more clothe you, O you of little faith? Therefore do not worry, saying, 'What shall we eat?' or 'What shall we drink?' or 'What shall we wear?' For after all these things the Gentiles seek. For your heavenly Father knows that you need all these things. But seek first the kingdom of God and His righteousness, and all these things shall be added to you. Therefore do not worry about tomorrow, for tomorrow will worry about its own things. Sufficient for the day is its own trouble.'* Matthew 6:25-34

I knew my mindset location (like the puppy) had to change, so I went silently upstairs to my bedroom in tears and lay on the bed reminding the Lord of His promises. While I was there I heard the front doorbell ring downstairs. I heard one of my kids open the door and two women came into our kitchen. They were in the kitchen for about 10 minutes.

I then heard them leave and after this I sensed a great peace in the house. I went downstairs and opened the door into the kitchen and I'll never forget what I saw in front of me. There were bags and bags of groceries all over the kitchen floor! We had food for not just the weekend but for the next two weeks – Glory to the Lord!

I never got to answer the question my wife asked. "Where is your God now?" God answered for me!

Gods' cattle refers to an avenue of making money! Let me explain... the majority of people will see cattle as animals that eat grass and lays about most days. But a farmer sees cattle way beyond that! They will see the cattle can breed more cattle = money! Or they can be slaughtered and sold to the butcher = money!
How do you see what is in front of you?

Our organisation, that helps churches and businesses advance, has a mission statement, that mission statement is Jeremiah 33:3; *'Call to Me, and I will answer you, and show you great and mighty things, which you do not know.'*

In fact the name of the organisation is *33Plus3*, based on that verse. Everything in our organisation is rooted in the belief; God is seeking to tell you and I things that we do not already know. It is those things that will make the difference in our lives. Let me conclude this part with this... If you are doing what you know to do and are ending up with the same results you always have, then like for the puppy, you need to at least move the bowl a little, change your thinking with doing, and it will change the results. Call upon the Lord today and He will answer you!

I am certain that not only is He the *God of perfect timing,* with my groceries arriving, but I am also certain of God manifesting His Word, *'I will meet all your needs,'* (Philippians 4:19) this increased my faith in Him. This pattern of the Lord's provision went on for a period of time.

Calling on the Lord for direction is a major key in turning your life around!

Tax reconciliation...

Before becoming a Christian, I always thought that businesses were set up to make money and the government bodies, especially the tax people, were in it to take their money away.

When I became born-again, God laid it on my heart to face the demon of tax. For me it was a fear, one that I had ran from for many years, and for many years my accountant had been telling me that I had potentially a large Capital Gains Tax liability from various disposals made in the past.

I decided to face this fear, come clean and go to Revenue. I had not filed a tax return for over 10 years. I went to the local Revenue office and collected tax return forms for all the years that I had not filed. I filled them up as best I could and then contacted the Collector Generals office in Limerick to make an appointment.

I travelled to Limerick for the appointment, bringing all the tax returns with me. I met the inspector who took me into a small meeting room where I proceeded to confess everything to her, I told her what had happened to me. I presented her with all my forms and to my astonishment she tore them up in front of me and put them in a bin!

She produced fresh forms from her file and said we should fill them up together. She asked me numerous questions as she filled in each of the forms. As she completed each form she gave it to me, asking me to read the information she had inserted and requesting me to sign it. I signed each form as we went through the process.

I told her what my accountant had been saying and she said that this was now dealt with in the returns completed. At the end of the meeting she said she would take the forms away and process them. She asked me to ring her in 10 days and thanked me for coming forward.

I spent the next 10 days praying but expecting another large bill which I would be unable to repay.

I rang her on the 10th day as she requested and she told me that she had just reconciled all the returns and was sending me a balancing statement for all the years. She said that there was good news and that I was getting a tax refund of €10k! I could not believe it and to this day I do not understand how this occurred. I am now a qualified tax consultant and I still do not know how this was made possible. It was a miracle – Glory to the Lord!

Learn to discern the true cause of fear, for at the other side of it dwells your freedom from it.

Instead of me running from government bodies, I have learned, they have been a blessing to me in the years since then, helping and advising accordingly.

Shortly after this, a representative from *The Irish Grocers Benevolent Fund* came to me to tell me that they would like to offer me financial support. He told me that the directors of the fund appreciated the contribution that I had made to their retail businesses during the time I had the business of my own that I sold in 1983.

This was such an encouragement to me at that time as now, though I was working through failure, I was receiving honour from my peers. They gave me €180 per week for about 18 months from that date. I was also supported by St Vincent de Paul in various ways during this time. Through this, I was learning to trust the Lord as my provider and I was learning how helpless I am without Him.

> **Value money otherwise it will slip through your hands when you don't! Ask yourself "Do I really need it?" Instead of convincing yourself... "I need to spend!"**

During this period, I found myself with a financial abundance for our day-to-day living despite the fact I still had all this debt hanging round me. I found it difficult to accept and enjoy this provision for a while but came to realise that this was the promises of God being fulfilled in my life as His child.

While all this was happening, I still was very aware and fearful of the magnitude of the circumstances that surrounded me. I found my only comfort was when I read the Bible as it seemed to be speaking to me words of comfort.

I was captured by the story of Jesus and his disciples before He ascended back to Heaven. He told them not to leave Jerusalem until He sent the comforter...

'On one occasion, while he was eating with them, he gave them this command: Do not leave Jerusalem, but wait for the gift my Father promised, which you have heard me speak about. For John baptized with water, but in a few days you will be baptized with the Holy Spirit.' Acts 1:4-5

This fascinated me as to why He told them to do this. As I reflected on this, I began to realise how fearful it must have been for the disciples to be in Jerusalem. Things were very dangerous for them there as anyone who was a follower of Jesus was likely to be killed.

Consider your time! You must allow time for projects to be developed. When a seed is planted it does not spring forth overnight. The same with any business, there's a time where one may need to work a lot of hours to create something but a day comes when the seed springs forth and a flower appears.

As the disciples were waiting on 'time' in the Upper Room, the Comforter (Holy Spirit) came at Pentecost and we can see from the account in the Bible that the disciples were totally and utterly transformed through the anointing of the Holy Spirit, to such an extent that the people thought they were drunk! They had such boldness and were not afraid any more.

When I read and reflected on all of this, I had a huge desire to have what these disciples had received and I felt unable to cope with the challenges I was facing in my own strength. I also was aware that *'Jesus* Christ *is the same yesterday, today and forever.'* (Hebrews 13:8) I started calling out to God each day to give me the same power that He gave His disciples at Pentecost, but I was not expecting what was about to take place.

One day, feeling very low and sad, I was in my sitting room crying out to God. I opened the Bible randomly and came to the part where

Jesus told us not to worry about what we eat or drink or the clothes we wear. He said; *"Look at the birds of the air."* (Matthew 6:26) As I read, I looked out my front window at the tree in the garden, I noticed it was full of birds.

At that moment I felt the atmosphere in the room change. I saw a dim red light come towards me from the far corner of the room and as it did, I felt like a bucket of warm oil was being poured over my head and flowing down over my body.

Even though there were so many challenges still facing me, as the anointing flowed I could feel all of the stress and anxiety lift out of my body. In that moment I felt totally changed and had a confidence that everything was going to be alright.

Being touched by God is one thing, but I was about to learn that I was being directed by Him. As Scripture states; *'For My thoughts are not your thoughts, Nor are your ways My ways," says the* L`ORD`*. "For as the heavens are higher than the earth, So are My ways higher than your ways, And My thoughts than your thoughts.'* Isaiah 55:8-9

The Lord has a plan...

'Trust in the Lord with all your heart, And lean not on your own understanding; In all your ways acknowledge Him, And He shall direct your paths.' Proverbs 3:5-6 (NKJV)

When a house is being rebuilt, there are normally some walls knocked down, things moved, extensions made etc. But in reality, before the house is made into something beautiful, it normally becomes a dump, filled with bricks, woodcuttings, waste pipes etc. Consider all these things laying where they should not be. But as asked earlier... "How do you see?" Do you see the house messed up or do you see a house being revamped for something better?

When God started to build my life, people could have said, 'Look at him, the millionaire who is now living in a St Vincent de Paul rented property.' But just as Jesus started in a stable, Liam McNamara can start in a St Vincent de Paul property.

Don't focus on those who are seeking to beat you down with their words, their gaze and of course their gossip. Discipline yourself to focus that God is bigger than them. I really sensed God was directing me at this time. I was being provided for but I needed to be working again and the job came, one that I was not expecting. I was offered a position selling life insurance on a commission only basis, nothing much to shout about, I hear you say, and I said the same. Previously I was of the opinion that life insurance sales reps were never really interested in people, but only in the money that they could make from them. However, because this door was opening for me, I had to choose between going in with an attitude of 'you're in it for the money' or 'is there a just cause for life insurance?' Therefore, my attitude needed an adjustment. I knew nothing about insurance and certainly did not know how to sell it!

In obedience to the Lord, I agreed to take up the position on the following Monday. However, the first obstacle hit me. I was advised by my future boss that I needed to have a car and obviously some cash to keep me going. The insurance company knowing my situation had agreed to pay me on account payments once I started, while I was in training and this would be deducted from my commissions once I earned them. It was an answer to prayer but I still didn't have a car and did not have enough money to travel to work. All I could do was to pray.

It was on the Saturday before I was due to start, a Christian friend of mine rang me to say that the Lord was speaking to him in prayer time about me and he felt I needed help with transport. He told me that another friend was on his way to Dublin with one of his cars which he said he was giving me for a while, if it would help. He was shocked when I told him what was happening with work and knew then that the Lord was speaking to him on this. I now had transport to start my new job!

Later that day another friend of mine rang me and jokingly said to me that I must have plenty of money. I asked why this should be so? He said he had a cheque for €65 belonging to me for some work I had done for him and he had been waiting for me to collect it. I never knew of this until then. I immediately went and collected the cheque and now I had transport to take up my job and had €65 in my pocket. God was answering my need!

> **Business people... When a client offers you the money take it, never refuse! For you do not know what tomorrow holds for you or the client. Instead of chasing money later, it is wiser to accept it now!**

I had no idea what plan the Lord had for me in this, but in faith and obedience I went with what was placed before me. I must confess that I had a deep sense when I was taking up this position that I was in the process spiritually of moving from wilderness to His promised land.

This was 28 years ago and I have no doubts today that it was such a time for My Lord to bring me to a new place and for His purpose.

Little did I know what started out as a 'seed,' walking into an opening that God gave me, a job I did not even want as an insurance salesman, actually evolved into a family business providing accountancy, business advisory, tax and financial services. God has truly blessed me and my family on this journey. Yet, even with God opening the door, I had to, in a sense, reinvent myself through training and education and secure qualifications in these subject matters. Scripture tells us, *'And be not conformed to this world, but be transformed by the renewing of your mind.'* (Romans 12:12) Renewing of the mind, does not mean just being able to quote Scripture but to know where God wants to lead you and be the best at it. In other words, if He has called you to be a musician, then seek to be the best you can be at it, hang out with others who are better than you, (Proverbs 27:17), buy books, learn ways of being better and then develop you, meaning you will think differently.

 **Decide to be your best at something!**

Release from debt...

It took approximately five years for the Lord to work out the fullness of my release from the huge debts that I had built up.

I had two events that signalled the conclusion of my indebtedness. The first of these was in 1993 which is five years after the failure of my business. The owner of the venture capital company that had invested in my business rang me and asked if I would meet him.

I went to his office where he explained a predicament that he had. He was selling his company but could not do so as there was an outstanding matter on file which related to me. He presented me with a letter that was written to his company by my solicitor stating an intention to issue proceedings against his company. I had forgotten about this letter but on seeing it, I remembered how this came about.

One of the banks with whom I had significant debt and had signed personal guarantees had told me at the time of the collapse that they were unhappy about how the venture capital company had handled their dealings with my company. They advised me that if I would issue proceedings against this company they would not call in my guarantees.

Even though I had no intention of taking this company on with a legal challenge, but because I needed to satisfy the bank, my solicitor wrote a letter notifying them of my intention to sue. The bank at that time were happy to drop my personal guarantees when they received this letter. This was the same letter that the owner of the Venture Capital company presented to me. He asked what it would take to settle this matter so that he could sell his company.

I was in shock and did not know what to say. I eventually told him that it would be a great blessing to my family if they could own a home again. He asked how much I would need for this. I felt led to ask him for what I regarded as a reasonable deposit. I asked him for €50k and he immediately wrote me a cheque for this amount and wished me well.

I left his office as if time had slowed down, trying to figure out what had just happened. I knew it was the Lord's blessing and I was really excited!

Immediately though, I started thinking that this amount would be of no value as I needed to be able to get a mortgage to buy a house. As my home had been repossessed, I knew I would be unable to obtain a mortgage.

I started to pray and asked the Lord what I should do. I then remembered I had a good friend who knew my situation and was the manager of a building society. I went to him and told him what was happening. I asked if he thought I might get a mortgage again after a repossession. He said it would all depend on my credit rating. I asked him to check on his systems. He did and to my astonishment my credit rating was clean and there was no record of my repossession. Glory to God!

I was able to get a mortgage and bought a home again for my family.

The second significant event came a few years later. Some of the collateral provided to the bank for my business was land, some of which was owned by myself and more that was owned by my mother. When the business collapsed all this collateral was called upon by the bank. This caused a lot of tension with my family. All my mother was interested in was that I would be alright. This is truly a mother's love.

Several years later, I happened to meet somebody that I used to know but had not seen for a long time. We sat and chatted and shared what we had been doing since we last met. He told me that he was working for the bank that had taken control of the collateral that I detailed earlier. I told him about my business collapse and felt led to express my curiosity as to whatever happened to the land. He offered to check for me.

The following day he rang me and told me that if I would go to a particular branch of the bank, there was an envelope there for me to collect. I went and collected all the deeds of the land that the bank had seized. They reside in my solicitors safe to this day – Glory to the Lord!

He truly is our restorer! I was gaining back all that had been lost, it was just as I had read in Deuteronomy 30; *'God, your God, will restore everything you lost; he'll have compassion on you; he'll come back and pick up the pieces from all the places where you were scattered. No matter how far away you end up, God, your God, will get you out of there and bring you back to the land your ancestors once possessed. It will be yours again. He will give you a good life and make you more numerous than your ancestors.'* (MSG)

Through all these years I have witnessed and experienced how the Lord took me from where I was when I met Him to where I am today. When I look back, I see that it took about five years for the Lord to bring me to freedom from the debts I had created. One of the big milestones on this journey was being able to buy my own home again after having lost our dream home.

One of the attitudes that I developed when I came to know the Lord was in relation to property and assets. It did not matter to me whether I owned assets or not or whether I owned a home or not. This was a key part of my freedom. All that was important to me was and still is, that I am in the centre of the Lord's plan for my life. He owns all of the world's assets anyway and He only wants the best for me.

'For every beast of the forest is Mine, And the cattle on a thousand hills.' Psalm 50:10 (NKJV)

'The silver is Mine, and the gold is Mine,' says the Lord of hosts.' Haggai 2:8 (NKJV)

Through this part of my journey, I came to experience what freedom felt like. Throughout my life up to this time I was brought up in a culture that regards success as just one step away from failure. So the fear of failure was always in front of me. Now I was experiencing the freedom that we have in Jesus.

'Stand fast therefore in the liberty by which Christ has made us free, and do not be entangled again with a yoke of bondage.' Galatians 5:1

CHAPTER THREE
The money world...

When I came into the world of finance and money and began to develop an understanding of its infrastructure, design and control, I became intrigued at what I was learning and what the Bible had to say about the matter. I found that there was a lot of prophesy in the Bible concerning what I saw and also the journey we are on as we go towards the end times. Some of this was a shock to me and took me some time to understand. The Lord promises to protect us on this journey. If you are surprised by what I am about to share with you, bear in mind what the Lord promised us as his children...

'Because you have made the Lord, who is my refuge, Even the Most High, your dwelling place, No evil shall befall you, Nor shall any plague come near your dwelling; For He shall give His angels charge over you, To keep you in all your ways. In their hands they shall bear you up, lest you dash your foot against a stone. You shall tread upon the lion and the cobra, The young lion and the serpent you shall trample underfoot.' Psalm 91:9-13

There are two currencies in this life! Faith and money. You cannot live in the spiritual world without the currency of faith, and you cannot live in the natural world without the currency of money. To succeed you MUST understand both currencies!

What faith is in our spiritual life, money is in our natural life, they are both currencies and they are such an intrinsic part of our lives. The surplus of money can easily create greed and selfishness and the lack of it can place us in bondage and damage us in so many ways. Our attitude towards money is of such importance that Jesus even referred to it;

'No servant can serve two masters; for either he will hate the one and love the other, or else he will be loyal to the one and despise the other. You cannot serve God and mammon.' Luke 16:13 (NJKV)

He actually refers 'money' to 'mammon' and also as a potential master. But who or what is mammon? I have researched this in some depth over the years and have come to understand that mammon is the spirit of love for money. Mammon seeks to accumulate money and wealth through greed and avarice. It is also one of satan's most powerful generals.

I can identify with that as it controlled me for so many years. I will develop this further.

The origin of money...

First, let us look at how money came about. In earliest times we read in the Bible that the currency used was silver, gold, land, crops and herds of animals to meet their needs. Wealth was usually reflected by the extent to which their barns were full of things like grain, hay and other such commodities and also by the size of their herds.

'Abram had become very wealthy in livestock and in silver and gold.' Genesis 13:2

This system evolved into more use of precious metals such as gold and silver as a means of paying for goods. This further evolved to where the Romans used leather to trade and later the British

Empire used whiskey and tobacco as a means of trading. These all had intrinsic value in those times. These systems are often referred to as '*commodity money.*'

As time evolved, Governments started to introduce what is called '*fiat money.*' This was in the form of paper or coin which made it much easier to transact. This paper was historically connected to a gold or silver standard which meant that the paper could be redeemed for a predetermined amount of gold or silver.

Interestingly, China was the first to introduce *fiat money* in the 10th century. Unfortunately, this collapsed after several years as the Government did not honour redemption of the paper when presented.

Europe introduced this system in the 12th century where a feudal system of government existed. The feudal system was based on a landlord and tenant system. Tenants used to store their wealth with the landlords for safekeeping and be given paper to acknowledge the value of what was placed in safekeeping.

Of course wars used to break out and the goods in safekeeping would be used by the landlords for war and they would then renege on the paper notes given to those who entrusted their wealth with them.

This evolved into the emergence of formal institutions where people could invest their money and wealth in safekeeping. Today these are called banks. These banks, coming to realise that not all the money given to them for safekeeping would be recovered at the same time, encouraged legislation to be introduced which allowed the banks to lend up to 90% of this money to others and charge interest on this, thereby making profit. This is called '*fractional banking.*' This was the cause of the bank collapse in Ireland in 2008 when the banks recklessly lent this money to others who could not repay it. This is why Ireland had a financial bailout.

From 2003 to 2008 the Irish economy had unprecedented growth with no unemployment and double-digit growth figures, it was a period in Irish economic history often referred to as *The Celtic Tiger*. This growth was driven mainly by the property market which resulted in a bubble that eventually burst. This caused chaos that eventually resulted in the banks running out of money, which required the International Monetary Fund in the EU to bail out the Irish Government who in turn bailed out the banks.

We need to realise that, in our situation in Ireland, it is those who paid for the bailout that are those whose money the banks were holding and had now lost. The other institutions – Banks were not affected and they are known as the *bond holders*.

Today we use paper money, credit cards and electronic banking which is based on currency such as the euro, dollar etc. We need to examine the actual value of these currencies.

Historically they were what they call 'legal tender' which basically means that they could be redeemed for a certain amount of gold, which provided wealth just as in the Old Testament. Today many of the currencies have no redeemable value and are in effect just pieces of paper.

The greatest example of this is the US dollar which up until 1973, could be redeemed if presented to the FED for a certain amount of Gold. This was declared on the dollar bill. Since 1973 by order of President Nixon, this was removed which meant that it became worthless in real terms.

Most people will also be aware that many currencies are traded against the dollar and commodity prices such as oil are priced, bought and sold in US dollar.

Why is currency so important?

It is important because it is the basis by which we can trade, ie. buy or sell. Look now at the following Scripture...

'It also forced all people, great and small, rich and poor, free and slave, to receive a mark on their right hands or on their foreheads, so that they could not buy or sell unless they had the mark, which

is the name of the beast or the number of its name.' Revelation 13:16-17

I promised earlier I would get back to mammon.

As Christians we should know that Jesus will eventually come back when the harvest is completed to defeat the antichrist who has clearly, by that stage, taken control of the wealth of the world. Jesus has already defeated satan through His death and resurrection. I will develop this further in the next chapter.

The main tool for satan to use is money which is under the spirit of mammon.

Inflation...

The use of *fiat money* will always give rise to inflation. One of the interventions used by governments to deal with the recent economic crash was to introduce '*quantitative easing*.'

This effectively means the printing circulation of large volumes of paper money which has no value. This has a feel-good response which is guaranteed to create significant inflation later as this feel-good attitude will cause prices to go up because people have more paper to spend and the banks start lending at high interest rates. So, the cycle starts all over again.

'*And I heard a voice in the midst of the four living creatures saying, "A quart of wheat for a denarius, and three quarts of barley for a denarius; and do not harm the oil and the wine.'* Revelation 6:6 (NKJV)

A denarius at that time was equivalent to a day's wages. Now that seems like hyper-inflation to me! Hyper-inflation is a situation where currency loses its value resulting in prices sky rocketing. The printing of paper as has been done, which has no value, is guaranteed in time to cause hyper-inflation. This is an economic fact.

The reason why Governments did this was because it would have defaulted in the huge debt it owed and its inability to repay it. Such a default would have caused a further economic collapse globally. In a sense all they were doing was *'kicking the can down the road.'* The hope in doing so, was economic growth would have rescued us out of the mess. This has not happened to date.

Recession or wealth transfer?

If we examine the major recessions which have occurred throughout the world historically including our own, you will see although it was spoken of as recession and believed to be so by most of us, the fact is, it is really wealth transfer. Assets and wealth owned by people having to be sold or repossessed by banks were acquired by others at huge discounts. Some of the very wealthy amongst us today are on record that they acquired the assets that eventually gave them their wealth in times of recession.

Let us examine the property crash that we have recently experienced. Many have had their homes repossessed by the banks. The banks then sell the property for whatever they can get. This means that others who have money can buy this property at *fire sale prices*.

In time this property becomes much more valuable to the new owner than the one who lost it, especially since he bought it in a *fire sale*. This demonstrates how the wealth originally belonging to the original owner was transferred to the new owner.

Good profitable businesses collapse into receivership because of cash flow and are bought by competitors and others at nominal values. The new owners are then able to restore the business to full profitability. This is wealth transfer.

Let's examine the stock market. Here people buy and sell shares making and losing money. Most of the decisions to buy and sell are made based on expert commentary and opinion. This is in essence propaganda aimed at increasing or decreasing share price.

Today you can buy futures, derivatives which are all essentially bets on share value outcomes at set times. This means that you can make gains on share price gains or losses. This sounds very like gambling to me.

When you then look at the setting of interest rates by FED and ECB their mandate is to manage economies and supposedly inflation. It is clear that they manipulate our lives through their decisions. The ultimate agenda here is the control of the wealth of the world.

I once came across a statement made by famous Dutch banker, Rothschild, who was a renowned figure in the global banking world, Rothschild said:

"Give me control of a country's money and I care not who writes their laws."

We should not be surprised with all that I have shared. It is all in the Bible. We can be sure that the world economy and wealth is coming under the control of few and will ultimately come under the control of one – the antichrist. I see the people in this world trying to survive in this environment unaware that they are under such control and manipulation for an end-time purpose.

I firmly believe that as members of the body of Christ here on earth, we need to open our spiritual eyes to see what is happening. I have become acutely aware of what is going on, through my own business and the insight it has given me, and through the time I have taken over the years to study this.

It is my experience that most Christians do not like to consider this, mainly because they are in ignorance of God's wisdom on the subject and fearful. Remember the promise of God for us...

'Because you have made the Lord, who is my refuge, Even the Most High, your dwelling place, No evil shall befall you, Nor shall any plague come near your dwelling; For He shall give His angels charge over you, To keep you in all your ways. In their hands they shall bear you up, lest you dash your foot against a stone. You shall tread upon the lion and the cobra, The young lion and the serpent you shall trample underfoot.' Psalms 91:9-13 (NKJV)

CHAPTER FOUR

Seeing the money world as a Christian...

In the previous chapter I shared what I have learned about the money world, it's purpose, operation and end-time agenda. For someone reading about this for the first time you might find it challenging. I know I used to. However, I always had an attitude that Jesus knows all and more about what is going on and knows well how to guide and protect His children through this environment. Indeed, He has promised to do so as we previously read in Psalms 91:9-13; *'He will keep you in all your ways.'*

Let us examine how God originally intended it to be.

First of all, God created us in His image and likeness and He gave man dominion over the earth and all therein so that they may rule.

'Then God said, "Let us make mankind in our image, in our likeness, so that they may rule over the fish in the sea and the birds in the sky, over the livestock and all the wild animals, and over all the creatures that move along the ground." So God created mankind in his own image, in the image of God he created them; male and female he created them.' Genesis 1:26-27

What does Dominion Mean?

Through this He gave man authority to rule. His instruction to man was to be fruitful and multiply. As we continue to read in Genesis 1:28; *'God blessed them and said to them, "Be fruitful and increase in number; fill the earth and subdue it. Rule over the fish in the sea and the birds in the sky and over every living creature that moves on the ground."'*

Here we see at the beginning of creation that God creates man in His image and likeness and gives him dominion over all the earth. Giving him dominion meant that He gave man, in the person of Adam, complete authority over this earth and all things in it and on it.

In doing this, God handed over or delegated His authority here on earth to Adam. So in a sense, God *the landlord* gave man *the tenant*, a lease over the earth.

With God being the landlord (owner) of the earth, we're the tenants. How are you looking after what the landlord has given to you?

So what happened?

When I became aware of this I was shocked. Look at what happened to Jesus when He encountered satan when He came to earth.

'Again, the devil took Him up on an exceedingly high mountain, and showed Him all the kingdoms of the world and their glory. And he said to Him, "All these things I will give You if You will fall down and worship me.' Matthew 4:8-9

How did satan come to have such authority to be able to offer Jesus all the kingdoms of the world?

He robbed it from Adam and Eve when they sinned in the garden. He usurped the authority given by God to Adam and Eve. He usurped the lease God gave to Adam over the earth.

People will say – 'Ah but that was before Jesus defeated satan through His death and resurrection.' Allow me to show you another Scripture...

'If the Good News we preach is hidden to anyone, it is hidden from the one who is on the road to eternal death. Satan, who is the god of this evil world, has made him blind, unable to see the glorious light of the Gospel that is shining upon him or to understand the amazing message we preach about the glory of Christ, who is God.' 2 Corinthians 4:3-4 (TLB)

Here in verse four we read that satan is the god of this evil world. This amazed me when I saw it first. This means we live in territory under the control of our enemy satan. But Scripture also tells us the following...

'For every beast of the forest is Mine, And the cattle on a thousand hills.' Psalm 50:10 (NKJV)

'The silver is Mine, and the gold is Mine,' says the Lord of hosts.' Haggai 2:8 (NKJV)

What's going on?

When satan tempted Adam and Eve, he forcefully took authority and caused them to sin. He then secured dominion over the earth.

Jesus came to take back this usurped authority from satan and restore it to those who are His people. This dominion and authority has been restored to all of us who are saved by the blood of Jesus. We can take it back from satan under the authority and power of the name of Jesus.

'For this reason Christ is the mediator of a new covenant, that those who are called may receive the promised eternal inheritance— now that he has died as a ransom to set them free from the sins committed under the first covenant.' Hebrews 9:15

Until Jesus comes back to lock him up, satan is still here and will remain here with his agenda. Until then, we live on earth where satan continues to have a stronghold. This means we live in a territory occupied by an enemy. This is why the Bible tells us we live in a *spiritual battlefield*. (Ephesians 6:12)

We have victory over the enemy occupying this territory and have a weapon greater than any of his weapons. It is the name of Jesus, whose power no foe can withstand.

This situation often puzzled me. I remember asking the Lord why He didn't lock satan up when He defeated him, I also queried, why He allows him to continue to roam and control the earth. I sensed Him say that if He did as I had queried, man would not have a choice any more. This made perfect sense to me.

You see we live in what is called the *church age*, which is the period that started when Jesus ascended up to Heaven and will end when He returns to set up His throne in Jerusalem. During this period, it is the Lord's plan and desire that all would accept what He has done and be saved. He said that He will not return until the harvest is gathered. Until then, while it is the Lord's desire that all would be saved, each one of us has a choice. This is why the enemy continues to occupy God's earth.

The spiritual battlefield...

Let us look at what is going on from a spiritual perspective.

'For we do not wrestle against flesh and blood, but against principalities, against powers, against the rulers of the darkness of this age, against spiritual hosts of wickedness in the heavenly places.' Ephesians 6:12 (NKJV)

This is what we should be aware of daily. Failure to do so will leave us open to all kinds of attack. Many Christians are under such attack today but are unaware of what is going on. Some are even blaming God.

In our natural world, if you are in a battlefield and you are unaware of what is going on, you are at risk of getting hurt or indeed getting killed. You would be unlikely to put yourself in such danger, so why do we put ourselves in such spiritual danger?

We have been warned in the Scriptures that we are in a spiritual battlefield. We have also been told how to secure victory in this battlefield.

In our flesh we operate using our senses ie. sight, smell, hearing, touch and taste. None of these are relevant when we deal with the spiritual realm. We must, therefore, develop an ability and a knowledge of how to deal with an enemy who operates in the spiritual realm. This is why the Bible tells us that our battle is not against flesh and blood but against spiritual forces. We need to have our spiritual eyes open to see what is going on around us and sometimes in front of us.

In order to operate through and against us, satan needs flesh. He needed to operate through a serpent to tempt Adam and Eve, resulting in them sinning. He is still doing it today and most of us do not see it.

According to Ephesians 6, we live in a spiritual battlefield. A battlefield is a place where someone tries to take your life, to imprison you. The devil is defeated in Christ, but is he defeated in your life?

I have already outlined how this evolved and how satan usurped the authority given to Adam by God. The battle we fight is to take back dominion over what God gave to His children.

God gave His children (Israel) the promised land but they had to claim it and fight for it in order to receive it. It is the same for us today. I meet many Christians who have great difficulty in understanding this. Most of them only think and assess from a natural perspective which means that if they cannot see it, hear it, touch it, smell it or taste it then it is not happening.

'We must open our spiritual eyes to be aware of what is going on.'

Assume that I just landed here on earth from outer space and landed in Aleppo in Syria totally unaware that there was a war going on, would you consider that I might be in danger?

I would certainly be shocked with what I would see going on around me with all the buildings collapsed, the people homeless, injured and traumatised and even lying dead on the streets. Because I had become aware of my surroundings I would come to realise that there must be a battle taking place and I am caught up in the middle of it. I would almost certainly attempt to escape from the environment, find shelter and protect myself. If I didn't attempt to protect myself then my life would be at risk.

Now look at what is going on around you today. You will see the same carnage and destruction of life with homelessness, suicide, rape, murder and abuse. This is not caused by an earthly war but by a spiritual war reigned on us by satan.

'Be sober, be vigilant; because your adversary the devil walks about like a roaring lion, seeking whom he may devour.' 1 Peter 5.8 (NKJV)

We cannot defeat the devil in our own strength. We must learn to be led by the Spirit into battles. Many Christians can walk with God but it's only being in God that the devil will remain defeated in our lives.

There are many times in my life where I have been faced with financial challenges that are much bigger than I am able to deal with. I am usually acutely aware of the spiritual attack that is facing me when this happens. I have come to know that it is not God's will that His people have these financial challenges and is, therefore, usually an attack of the enemy.

God wants us to prosper...

'Beloved, I pray that you may prosper in all things and be in health, just as your soul prospers.' 3 John 1:2 (NKJV)

'For I know the thoughts that I think toward you, says the Lord, thoughts of peace and not of evil, to give you a future and a hope. Then you will call upon Me and go and pray to Me, and I will listen to you. And you will seek Me and find Me, when you search for Me with all your heart.' Jeremiah 29:11-13 (NKJV)

I should point out that sometimes we can leave doors open that enables satan to attack us. I will develop this further when I share about stewardship.

When we are faced with a financial crisis, I have come to see both in myself and in others, that we naturally react in either of two ways:

- We become paralysed and unable to respond because of fear, confusion and uncertainty.
- We start striving to fix it and end up exhausted, in bad health and in many cases suffering a form of, or, an actual breakdown.

None of these methods work!

The reason they will not work is because you are under spiritual attack and to succeed you must fight with spiritual weapons and not flesh. I will go through the steps that we need to take to gain victory with our spiritual weaponry in the following chapters.

The Scriptural references for this are...

'Finally, my brethren, be strong in the Lord and in the power of His might. Put on the whole armour of God, that you may be able to stand against the wiles of the devil.' Ephesians 6:10-11 (NJKV)

'Stand therefore, having girded your waist with truth, having put on the breastplate of righteousness, and having shod your feet with the preparation of the gospel of peace; above all, taking the shield of faith with which you will be able to quench all the fiery darts of the wicked one. And take the helmet of salvation, and the sword of the Spirit, which is the word of God.' Ephesians 6:14-17

'No weapon formed against you shall prosper, and every tongue which rises against you in judgment You shall condemn. This is the heritage of the servants of the LORD, and their righteousness is from Me," Says the LORD.' Isaiah 54:17 (NKJV)

'That at the name of Jesus every knee should bow, of those in heaven, and of those on earth, and of those under the earth,' Philippians 2:10 (NKJV)

In the next chapters, I have attempted to set out, both Scripturally and through my own experience, the environment that we as Christians need to be aware of as we journey through our lives as children of the living God here on earth.

The rest of this book will now focus on the steps to victory in dealing with and taking authority over money in our lives.

CHAPTER FIVE

The bondage of debt...

Earlier I shared how satan is using money to take control of the world's wealth and people. Ultimately, if we read what the Bible tells us, we can see that all commercial life will be under his control. This is a time where the world will not be able to buy or sell if we do not carry the mark of the beast.

'And that no one may buy or sell except one who has the mark or the name of the beast, or the number of his name.' Revelation 13:17 (NKJV)

We must **always** be aware that God has promised us protection from this.

'And I heard a voice in the midst of the four living creatures saying, "A quart of wheat for a denarius, and three quarts of barley for a denarius; and do not harm the oil and the wine." Revelation 6:6 (NKJV)

The oil and the wine are those who are washed by the blood of Jesus (wine) and are filled with the Holy Spirit. (oil)

Money can also be used by satan to place people in bondage to others. If you own a property for example and I want to get this property off you, what is one of the current legitimate ways I could do so?

If I offer you money and encourage you to take it secured against the property and continue this process for a while until you are no longer able to repay the debt you owe me, you will then default and I will be able to repossess your property. But you might ask what about the money you lent? Are you not at a loss on this?

What if the money I gave you was not mine but belonged to others who had given it to me. Does this situation sound familiar? This is exactly what the banks have done during the Celtic Tiger era.

Scripture tells us that ideally, we should be free of debt.

'Owe no one anything except to love one another, for he who loves another has fulfilled the law.' Romans 13:8 (NKJV)

I believe that this word is given by way of advice rather than as a command. The reason I believe this is so, is because the Lord also told us to lend to others.

'But love your enemies, do good, and lend, hoping for nothing in return; and your reward will be great, and you will be sons of the Most High. For He is kind to the unthankful and evil.' Luke 6:35

If the Lord encourages us to lend, then if we are to receive from those who lend, we become borrowers. I believe if we borrow we must borrow wisely in line with Scripture.

'The rich rules over the poor, And the borrower is servant to the lender.' Proverbs 22:7 (NKJV)

'Do not be unequally yoked together with unbelievers. For what fellowship has righteousness with lawlessness? And what communion has light with darkness?' 2 Corinthians 6:14 (NKJV)

'For which of you, intending to build a tower, does not sit down first and count the cost, whether he has enough to finish it.' Luke 14:28 (NKJV)

I believe the lessons that these Scriptures give us are…

- Do not borrow beyond what you are **sure** you can repay.

- Carefully examine the financial consequences of your borrowing.
- Be at peace in your spirit in doing so, having prayed about it beforehand.
- Realise that just because the bank is willing to lend to you does not mean it is wise for you to accept it.

I know of many Christians today who either have or plan to file for bankruptcy as a means of escaping from debt. I am firmly of the view that it is not God's will that any of His children become bankrupt. Indeed, it is contrary to who He said we are in Him.

I believe it is a statement of unbelief in the promises of God to allow ourselves to become bankrupt.

A few years ago the wife of a Christian friend of mine in the UK rang me in tears telling me that herself and her husband were about to be made bankrupt by banks and creditors. I told her what I have just written about this kind of situation and furthermore that my wife and I had decided to travel to the UK to meet these people who were planning to put them in bankruptcy. I asked her to arrange meetings.

Before going to the meetings we prayed and asked the Lord to give us wisdom for a rescue plan that would avoid bankruptcy. He did just that and we went to the meetings armed with our plans.

When seeking advice, seek spiritual and natural advice. Ask your pastor/a trusted spiritual adviser (one who knows Biblical principles) and ask a professional person of that avenue.

The outcome of this was that arrangements were made for settlement, with debt written down and agreed and the matter concluded without the need for bankruptcy.

I should have been declared bankrupt many times over when my business collapsed but the Lord we serve is a faithful God who will protect and defend His children with all His might at **all** times.

We all would love to be debt-free as the Lord advises. Most of us continue to have to deal with debt in our lives. We live in a world economy that is based on debt. In my own life I became completely free of all the debt that trapped me. The freedom I experienced was amazing.

Sometimes we still can make a mistake, and a mistake will cause us to move off lane to a side lane, that can lead to another path, more debt! But a wise person will seek to return back into the main lane sooner rather than later. Whether it's a mistake or change of circumstances… Suddenly the landlord telling you that you have to leave his house that he now wants to sell. We must seek to create a buffer around our life for the 'suddenlies' of life… the car breaking down, a move of house, death, or just a wrong decision. I will share about this in more detail in another chapter. We must become careful to apply wisdom to any debt we take on.

We have all witnessed the property bubble bursting and subsequent bank collapse and many continue to suffer because of it today. In my business I meet with hundreds of people both Christian and non-Christian who are in bondage to debt and are unable to get free. Whether they are in a financial situation that is unrecoverable, or one that looks impossible to solve, we can advise them on a way out, I can introduce them to the best financial adviser in the world – Jesus Christ. Schooling and education gave me the knowledge of money culture but it was meeting Jesus Christ that gave me the understanding of the Kingdom culture of money. Rather than the enemy using it to destroy God's people, that which the devil had planned, God can turn it around if we listen and obey His voice and instructions. This is how I became free from the bondage of debt.

There are **three** steps that the Lord has taught me.

1. *Humble yourself to those whom you owe the money.*

Many have great difficulty with this as they are unable to take responsibility for their decision to take on the debt at the outset. They feel that the banks in some way were responsible and to blame. In a sense and in many cases they are right, as the banks did recklessly lend during this time. However, the offer of money when it is accepted by the individual makes them responsible for the debt. This is painful, but true.

Failure to take responsibility has caused huge problems between banks and individuals, which in most cases ends up in the legal arena, which never ends in the client's favour. From my experience in dealing with the banks on behalf of clients, I can confirm that one of the first questions the banks credit committees have on their checklist when assessing a case is; 'Is the customer cooperative and have they proactively engaged with the bank?'

Many people I meet have a difficulty in understanding what is meant by 'humbling yourself' and in some way get caught up in interpreting humbling oneself as within their rights as consumers or as humans. The best example of humbling oneself is given to us by Jesus himself. He had all the rights on His side and was who He said He was. Yet He chose not to attempt to exercise His rights so that we might be saved.

2. *Ask for mercy.*

This only becomes possible if you have taken responsibility. This is a biblical principle.

> '*When you go with your adversary to the magistrate, make every effort along the way to settle with him, lest he drag you to the judge, the judge deliver you to the officer, and the officer throw you into prison.*' Luke 12:58 (NKJV)

I have personal experience of this in my life. During my escape from debt I received a summons to court from the banks to secure a judgement against me for approximately €11k. This arose from my car finance for the company car I had in my previous business that collapsed.

At the time, I knew I would not be able to keep the car as I could not afford the repayments. I took the car back to the garage where I had originally purchased it and asked to see the manager. I gave him the keys telling him what had happened. He took me to his office and thanked me saying that in his time as manager, he had never seen anyone come and give the car back in such a situation.

He said he would do everything in his power to ensure that this would be the last I would hear of this. He wished me well and I left thanking the Lord for the favour I had just received from this man and believing in faith that the matter was concluded.

About 12 months later I received the summons from the bank with whom the car had been financed. You can imagine my thoughts - So much for the Lord's favour!

I had to go to a friend of mine who is a solicitor to represent me. He agreed to do so on the condition that I would allow him to deal with the bank on the matter. I agreed but it was obvious, however, that no defence could be offered to avoid the judgement. It was about a week before the court case that I had engaged with the solicitor.

I went through the next days troubled as so much debt had been settled by this time without court cases yet this matter was about to go to court for a small amount.

The court case was to be on a Tuesday, on the Wednesday of the previous week, I was in prayer when I came across the Scripture above. I really felt the Lord was prompting me to *'settle on the way.'*

I decided there and then to ring the bank manager whose name was on the summons letter. To my surprise, I got straight through to him. I told him who I was and of the court case the following week. I told him of my circumstances and asked him for mercy and in the name of God to forgive me. There was silence on the phone for what seemed like a long time. He then said; "Ring me back on Friday at 3pm," and put the phone down.

I had arranged a meeting for the Friday morning to prepare for the court. When I met the solicitor I confessed to him what I had done. He was annoyed with me and asked me what the manager had said. I told him what he had said to which he started to laugh at me as if I was crazy. I asked him if I could wait until that afternoon, so I could make the phone call before I decided how to proceed. He agreed.

I rang the bank manager as requested on the Friday afternoon and again got straight through to him. I told him who I was and of his request to ring him. He then told me to tell my solicitor that he did not need to attend court on the Tuesday as they were forgiving me the debt. He wished me and my family well for the future.

I told my solicitor and I think he is still trying to figure out what happened even though I told him about the Lord that I serve and His promises.

3. *Expect God's favour.*

The Lord has promised us favour in these situations. We must have faith and trust His Word on this. Here are some Scriptures on this...

'Trust in the Lord with all your heart, And lean not on your own understanding; In all your ways acknowledge Him, And He shall direct your paths.' Proverbs 3:5-6 (NKJV)

'Because you have made the LORD, who is my refuge, Even the Most High, your dwelling place, No evil shall befall you, Nor shall any plague come near your dwelling; For He shall give His angels charge over you, To keep you in all your ways. In their hands they shall bear you up, Lest you dash your foot against a stone.' Psalm 91:9-12 (NKJV)

'What then shall we say to these things? If God is for us, who can be against us.' Romans 8:31 (NKJV)

'No weapon formed against you shall prosper, And every tongue which rises against you in judgment You shall condemn. This is the heritage of the servants of the LORD, and their righteousness is from Me," Says the Lord.' Isaiah 54:17 (NKJV)

As I apply what the Lord has taught me, I see the same result time after time, which has resulted in the Lord using me to secure significant debt write off and favour from the banks on behalf of clients. God's Word can never go out and come back void. He can never lie! Therefore, His promise is always yes and amen for those who will put their trust in Him.

'God is not human, that he should lie, not a human being, that he should change his mind. Does he speak and then not act? Does he promise and not fulfil?' Numbers 23:19

Not a formula...

Many when reading this may see this as some kind of formula. That would be wrong. Each situation is different but God is **still** the same. The motive of the heart is so crucial to the outcome. If you try and apply these principles in some way, to use God for selfish purpose, then you will fail. Your motive should always be to deepen your relationship with Him, to serve Him better and more, having been set free from the bondage that debt holds you. As a child of God, we must learn to put all our trust in Him. That means we need to let go all that we have to Him.

In doing so, we need to realise that the One you are giving it all to, owns it all in the first place and wants to bless you and prosper you in **all** things. I have found that there is an incredible freedom that comes upon us in this. The world will challenge you on this and say that this is gross irresponsibility. The opposite is the case and it is the wisest decision you can make.

This was **the key to my financial breakthrough** and it will be yours also if you are prepared to put your trust in the One who created you, who knew you before you were formed in your mother's womb, who loves you enough to have given His life for you so that you could have life and life in abundance here on earth and then in heaven.

When you ponder and meditate on this you start to see the challenges you face in perspective. This brings hope and expectation that ends up with joy even though you may be still going through your challenges. The Lord will surely bring you into freedom in Him and glorify His name through your life here on earth so that others may know that He lives. Hallelujah!

Cycle of financial defeat used by satan

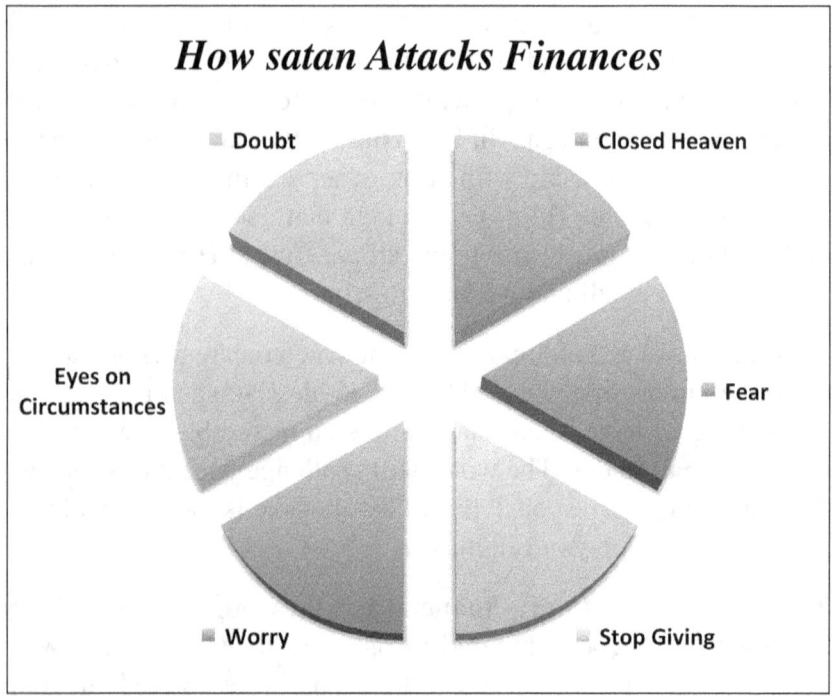

Dealing with fear...

I have witnessed through my financial business, the havoc that debt causes in people's lives. As you have read, I also know what it was like in my own personal situation. The first emotion that arises for most people is FEAR.

Fear of what is going to happen, fear of the unknown, fear of not knowing how to deal with the situation. It is a medically-proven fact that fear can cause health breakdown. So what starts as fear can end up with all kinds of health issues arising.

We need to know that fear is not of God but of satan and he does not want us to operate in faith. We all have situations that occur in our daily lives that trigger us to become fearful. We need to recognise what is happening quickly, otherwise we can easily become caught up with it.

Over the years, I was very fearful of the debt and hopelessness that surrounded me, I see that none of the things I feared came to pass. It was my imagination thinking of what might happen, that was the thing that made me fearful.

I feared that we would run out of money, have no food and I would see my children go hungry. I felt that I would never get a job again, especially as the industry I worked in had rejected me, verbally, physically and politically. These people were my classmates who had now rose to senior management positions in the big food companies. I believed my marriage was over and did not know the consequences this would have on our children. Yet, it survived for a further 15 years. I feared the public humiliation of bankruptcy, which I saw as inevitable. I feared the public spectacle of losing our big house. I found it difficult to cope with helplessness and hopelessness as I was always the one who found the solution.

Therefore, the fear was entirely in my mind and of my imagination.

I am convinced that this is why Jesus, when He was here on earth, so many times told His disciples; "Do not be afraid." Or; "Fear not."

He knew fear paralyses the person and effects the outcome.

When we are fearful we find it hard to focus. We find it hard to make decisions and be objective. I have seen a pattern at work in business which I am convinced is a tool of the enemy to destroy people's lives. Some of you reading this book may be in business and will appreciate what I am going to describe.

So your business is suffering cash flow problems and you are trying to cut costs and manage as best as you can. Because of the tightness of your cash flow, you are not paying your creditors on time and now they are starting to ring you and put pressure on you.

Then the bank contacts you and starts to review your facility with them, in some cases taking away your overdraft. You now have less money to work with, so you start to put pressure on your customers to pay you on time. These people are in the same place as you, only they don't tell you!

You now end up in a stressful relationship with your customers – the very people who are your lifeline. By the time you get to this place you are exhausted as you have been striving all this time trying to make ends meet and not wanting to disappoint anyone. You are stressed out and do not know where to turn, except to keep trying harder.

The icing on the cake here is where your relationship with your wife may not be the best and your current situation is not helping.

Does this sound familiar?

Let me share a Scripture that sets out exactly the situation I have described. This is the Scripture that the Lord showed me at an early stage of my journey and remains today the Scripture that I probably apply in my daily life more than any other. It is ingrained in my heart and I know it *off by heart* and speak it to myself regularly.

'For thus says the Lord GOD, the Holy One of Israel: "In returning and rest you shall be saved; In quietness and confidence shall be your strength." But you would not, And you said, "No, for we will flee on horses" – Therefore you shall flee! And, "We will ride on swift horses" – Therefore those who pursue you shall be swift! One thousand shall flee at the threat of one, At the threat of five you shall flee, Till you are left as a pole on top of a mountain And as a banner on a hill. Therefore the LORD will wait, that He may be gracious to you; And therefore He will be exalted, that He may have mercy on you. For the LORD is a God of justice; Blessed are all those who wait for Him. For the people shall dwell in Zion at Jerusalem; You shall weep no more. He will be very gracious to you at the sound of your cry; When He hears it, He will answer you. And though the Lord gives you the bread of adversity and the water of affliction, Yet

your teachers will not be moved into a corner anymore, But your eyes shall see your teachers. Your ears shall hear a word behind you, saying, "This is the way, walk in it," Whenever you turn to the right hand Or whenever you turn to the left.' Isaiah 30:15-21 (NKJV)

That first line reads... *'In returning and rest you shall be saved!'* In 'returning' is repentance; returning back to the original plan... Hearing from God and obeying Him! The word 'rest' in the original means – to rest in that direction, to stay focused on hearing from God and obeying, if we do this, then life will be so different for many of us!

Above all priorities in life, your main priority is to hear His voice. Make a practice of going to the quiet place and hearing the voice of the Lord!

Striving is the art of the flesh, it strives because it is only ever temporarily satisfied, and this Scripture is all about striving. Sometimes we speak about it as being at the rock face. If you are at the rock face and you keep hacking away at the rock without first looking at where you are hacking, you can bring the rock down on top of you!

If you apply the steps that I have outlined in this chapter and take the Scriptures into your heart, it will change your life and bring you into a freedom that you have not experienced before.

CHAPTER SIX

Wealth vs poverty...

This is a much talked-about and taught subject within churches. There is at one end, the prosperity gospel sometimes known as the *'name it and claim it'* gospel and at the other end, the gospel which speaks of our cross, piety etc. Let us look at what the Bible says about it.

Does God want us to be poor and in poverty?

'Who is the man that fears the Lord? Him shall he teach in the way He chooses. He himself shall dwell in prosperity, and his descendants shall inherit the earth.' Psalm 25:12-13 (NKJV)

'Therefore keep the words of this covenant, and do them, that you may prosper in all that you do.' Deuteronomy 29:9 (NKJV)

'Beloved, I pray that you may prosper in all things and be in health, just as your soul prospers.' 3 John 2 (NKJV)

'You shall eat in plenty and be satisfied, And praise the name of the LORD your God, Who has dealt wondrously with you; And My people shall never be put to shame.' Joel 2:26 (NKJV)

I have only shown you some references, the Bible is full of references, and when you see it is God's will for you to have and not to be in lack, then you will read the Bible looking down from being seated in Christ instead of looking up as a beggar. I believe it is reasonable for us to be convinced based on these Scriptures that the Lord wants us to prosper in all things including money.

What does the Lord say about Poverty?

'However, if you do not obey the LORD your God and do not carefully follow all his commands and decrees I am giving you today, all these curses will come on you and overtake you: You will be cursed in the city and cursed in the country. Your basket and your kneading trough will be cursed. The fruit of your womb will be cursed, and the crops of your land, and the calves of your herds and the lambs of your flocks.' Deuteronomy 28:15-18

These verses clearly describe poverty. These Scriptures also describe poverty as a curse. I believe poverty is a curse caused by disobedience. The following Scripture tells us that Jesus became a curse for us and fulfilled all the price for disobedience as set out in Deuteronomy...

"Cursed is anyone who makes an idol—a thing detestable to the Lord, the work of skilled hands—and sets it up in secret."

Then all the people shall say, "Amen!"

"Cursed is anyone who dishonors their father or mother."

Then all the people shall say, "Amen!"

"Cursed is anyone who moves their neighbor's boundary stone."

Then all the people shall say, "Amen!"

"Cursed is anyone who leads the blind astray on the road."

Then all the people shall say, "Amen!"

"Cursed is anyone who withholds justice from the foreigner, the fatherless or the widow."

Then all the people shall say, "Amen!"

"Cursed is anyone who sleeps with his father's wife, for he dishonors his father's bed."

Then all the people shall say, "Amen!"

"Cursed is anyone who has sexual relations with any animal."

Then all the people shall say, "Amen!"

"Cursed is anyone who sleeps with his sister, the daughter of his father or the daughter of his mother."

Then all the people shall say, "Amen!"

"Cursed is anyone who sleeps with his mother-in-law."

Then all the people shall say, "Amen!"

"Cursed is anyone who kills their neighbor secretly."

Then all the people shall say, "Amen!"

"Cursed is anyone who accepts a bribe to kill an innocent person."

Then all the people shall say, "Amen!"

"Cursed is anyone who does not uphold the words of this law by carrying them out."

Then all the people shall say, "Amen!" Deuteronomy 27:15-26 (NIV)

Now let us go to the New Testament and look at Galatians.

'Christ has redeemed us from the curse of the law, having become a curse for us (for it is written, "Cursed is everyone who hangs on a tree" that the blessing of Abraham might come upon the Gentiles in Christ Jesus, that we might receive the promise of the Spirit through faith.' Galatians 3:13-14 (NKJV)

Through what Jesus did we are set free from the curses of the law. That means we are free from the curse of poverty and the blessings are ours.

In Deuteronomy 28 we read; *'If you fully obey the Lord your God and carefully follow all his commands I give you today, the Lord your God will set you high above all the nations on earth. All these blessings will come on you and accompany you if you obey the Lord your God:'*

- *'You will be blessed in the city and blessed in the country.'*

- *'The fruit of your womb will be blessed, and the crops of your land and the young of your livestock—the calves of your herds and the lambs of your flocks.'*

- *'Your basket and your kneading trough will be blessed.'*

- *'You will be blessed when you come in and blessed when you go out.'*

- *'The Lord will grant that the enemies who rise up against you will be defeated before you. They will come at you from one direction but flee from you in seven.'*

- *'The Lord will send a blessing on your barns and on everything you put your hand to. The Lord your God will bless you in the land he is giving you.'*

- *'The Lord will establish you as his holy people, as he promised you on oath, if you keep the commands of the Lord your God and walk in obedience to him. Then all the peoples on earth will see that you are called by the name of the Lord, and they will fear you. The Lord will grant you abundant prosperity—in the fruit of your womb, the young of your livestock and the crops of your ground—in the land he swore to your ancestors to give you.'*

- *'The Lord will open the heavens, the storehouse of his bounty, to send rain on your land in season and to bless all the work of your hands. You will lend to many nations but will borrow from none. The Lord will make you the head, not the tail. If you pay attention to the commands of the Lord your God that*

I give you this day and carefully follow them, you will always be at the top, never at the bottom. Do not turn aside from any of the commands I give you today, to the right or to the left, following other gods and serving them.'

We can receive this freedom and blessings only through faith in what Jesus has done. This means we must believe it in our hearts to receive it. When we hear what the Lord wants us to do then we must be obedient. Not 'doing,' as in works, but in hearing and obeying.

The way we think is the way we believe and the way we believe is the way we act!

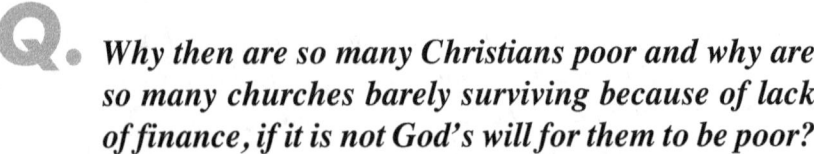

Why then are so many Christians poor and why are so many churches barely surviving because of lack of finance, if it is not God's will for them to be poor?

I've met so many Christians who have huge difficulty breaking free into the fullness of what God has promised. They know and believe what the Bible says but find it hard to accept that the promise is for them. Our culture and tradition plays a big part in this. Many of us have heard such sayings or even have said them as;

'Don't expect too much and you will never be disappointed.'

'The next step after success is failure.'

'Don't count your chickens before they are hatched.'

All of these represent a mindset that is not in line with the Word of God. In fact, these attitudes are tools of satan to keep us from walking in the fullness of God's promises.

I am speaking from experience as I write this, as I suffered for most of my life with a fear of failure which in hindsight affected many of my decisions and actions and also how I dealt with people. I lived on adrenalin as a means of getting through. I know this in particular, effected my relationship with people.

I believe there are two reasons why many Christians remain as they are;

1. *Unbelief.*

If we as Christians or as a church do not believe that God wishes to **prosper** us and that Jesus defeated the curse of poverty, then we will not have the faith to believe for our prosperity. We cannot walk in faith and unbelief at the same time. The meaning for unbelief is – to have not went far enough. And throughout the Bible this is shown many times, from the spies who went into the land to spy it out. They all tasted it but only two got to keep it, because the rest were afraid of the giants. My friend, God can open a great door of opportunity like He did for them and it is God's will for you to enter, BUT fear, the root of unbelief will NEVER let you inherit it!

> **When God opens a door – take the step! God never called you to work it out, He called you to obey and go through! Remember, it's not a flashlight onto your feet for distance, it's a lamp onto your feet, meaning one step at a time! (Psalms 119:105)**

Our unbelief will not change unless we choose to believe what God did for us, said to us and promised us. This is where we must exercise our faith which is, in itself, a gift from God, given to everyone who accepts Jesus as their Lord. It is therefore, not about trying to believe harder, but to allow His Word to rest deep in our hearts and trust Him to do what He said He would do.

2. *Deception.*

Our enemy satan is robbing us or holding back what God has given us.

'The thief comes only to steal and kill and destroy; I have come that they may have life, and have it to the full.' John 10:10

'Be sober, be vigilant; because your adversary the devil walks about like a roaring lion, seeking whom he may devour.' 1 Peter 5:8 (NKJV)

I believe it is because of this that God has promised us in Joel 2:25; *'So I will restore to you the years that the swarming locust has eaten.'*

We can also find in Daniel where the archangel Michael was delayed by satan and had to wrestle with the prince of Persia to bring Daniel his blessing.

We need to be aware of what might be going on as it may be stopping God's blessings in our lives. We must stand against all such attacks and realise that we have authority over satan in the name of Jesus. We must also check and ensure that we are walking in God's will in our circumstances.

Just because the answer is not in front of you, does not mean the answer is not on the way. Always give praise in the transition!

Let us now focus on God's promise of wealth in our lives and in our churches. I regularly find that when we focus on this, people immediately start to think of money.

They perceive that wealth is always measured by money. This is not so. I cannot find anywhere in the Bible where God promised specifically to give us money. What God did promise is that He would give us the power to get wealth!

'And you shall remember the LORD your God, <u>for it is He who gives you power to get wealth</u>, that He may establish His covenant which He swore to your fathers, as it is this day.' Deuteronomy 8:18 (NKJV)

There are a number of great examples in the Bible where God fulfilled this promise and which should encourage us to receive our blessing also.

Solomon was regarded as one of the wealthiest men in the world. This came about when God asked him what he would like to receive from Him. Most of us today would most likely ask for money or wealth. Solomon did not ask for either of these but instead asked for wisdom. It was this wisdom that made him so wealthy, that the Queen of Sheba came to him to understand how he was able to acquire such wealth. I will develop this further in the next chapter.

I want to encourage you at this point to agree to start to lay aside any *poverty mentality* that you might have. Start to take hold of the promises that the Lord has set before us.

'And my God shall supply all your need according to His riches in glory by Christ Jesus.' Philippians 4:19 (NKJV)

'The Lord is my shepherd; I shall not want. He makes me to lie down in green pastures; He leads me beside the still waters. He restores my soul; He leads me in the paths of righteousness For His name's sake.' Psalm 23:1-3

Breaking through and transforming your mind and thinking will not happen overnight. Your current attitudes and thoughts have been cultivated over many years and will not be changed in a day. As you start to change, you are likely to find that your financial situation may appear very challenging or indeed insurmountable and this becomes a source of discouragement to proceed. You need to realise what is going on.

You are in a spiritual battlefield where satan is controlling you through your finances and does not want to let go!

Your financial situation now looks like a mountain to climb. If you experience this, then I want to give you five steps to break free. These steps have helped me deal with many financial challenges during my life as a Christian...

YOUR TO DO LIST....

1. **Take time to reflect on who you are in Christ Jesus.**

    This will strengthen you as what He has said about you and how He sees you is so powerful and encouraging. He has your back!

2. **Switch from worrying and being focused on your circumstances**

    Train yourself to focus on Jesus and the miraculous power of Him. The more you look at your circumstances, the more satan will seek to influence you.

3. **Pray for yourself as you would do for others!**

    We can pray to God for what is a solution deemed as an impossibility for others. But when it comes to our situation, we become fearful. The same God you have prayed to for others is the same God you must believe can reach you. See your challenge as a miracle opportunity for God to prove Himself. After all, the impossible becomes possible through Him.

4. **Find His promises for you concerning your circumstances in His Word.**

    Read the Scriptures of how God broke through miraculously for His people in the Bible. How much more can He breakthrough for you today! He's the same yesterday, TODAY (right at this moment) and forever.

5. Take a step of faith on these promises.

Learn to step out of the boat, and walk towards the Master. Don't focus on failing, focus on that if you fail He is well able to lift you up again. (Matthew 14:22-33)

These steps **will never fail you** if you apply them. Be disciplined in their application.

CHAPTER SEVEN

Power to get wealth...

'And you shall remember the LORD your God, for it is He who gives you power to get wealth, that He may establish His covenant which He swore to your fathers, as it is this day.' Deuteronomy 8:18 (NKJV)

What is Wealth?

What does it mean to have wealth and what does it look like? I believe it is best described in the following Scripture:

'And God is able to make all grace abound toward you, that you, always having all sufficiency in all things, may have an abundance for every good work.' 2 Corinthians 9:8 (NKJV)

It is clear from this that the Lord's wealth covers all aspects of our life including money.

'A good man leaves an inheritance to his children's children, But the wealth of the sinner is stored up for the righteous.' Proverbs 13:22 (NKJV)

This tells us that not only will we have **all** sufficiency in **all** things, but we will have substance to leave an inheritance not just for our children but for our grandchildren.

In summary, we should have no lack in our lives here on earth, we should be in a position to abundantly support our church and have enough left over to be able to leave an inheritance to our grandchildren. Do you have an inheritance left aside for your children and your grandchildren? Or are you just surviving? Do you believe it is God's will for us to be overcomers in some things or all things? I hope you said, 'ALL THINGS!'

Q. *How do we start the journey to arrive at the place where the Lord said we should be?*

The key is to understand what God meant when He promised to give us the power to get wealth.

I believe there are two aspects to our wealth and these are our *spiritual wealth* and our *material wealth*. Both of these are inextricably linked and have been promised to us.

In both cases we must learn to take hold of the promises.

Success is primarily achieved through faith in the Lord Jesus Christ as our Saviour and His Lordship. We must learn to be totally surrendered to Him, learn to hear His voice and choose to trust His promises rather than be influenced by the circumstances facing us daily in our lives.

'Trust in the Lord with all your heart, And lean not on your own understanding; In all your ways acknowledge Him, And He shall direct your paths.' Proverbs 3:5-6 (NKJV)

In order to start out on the journey we should understand that wealth is not just about money as I have outlined earlier, so we need to stop focusing on money and instead focus on the opportunities that the Lord places before us.

There are a number of great examples in the Bible where men of God found fulfilment of His promises and which should encourage us to receive our blessing also.

Solomon...

Solomon was regarded as one of the wealthiest men in the world. This came about when God asked him what he would like to receive from Him.

'At Gibeon the Lord appeared to Solomon in a dream by night; and God said, "Ask! What shall I give you? And Solomon said: "You have shown great mercy to Your servant David my father, because he walked before You in truth, in righteousness, and in uprightness of heart with You; You have continued this great kindness for him, and You have given him a son to sit on his throne, as it is this day. Now, O Lord my God, You have made Your servant king instead of my father David, but I am a little child; I do not know how to go out or come in. And Your servant is in the midst of Your people whom You have chosen, a great people, too numerous to be numbered or counted. Therefore give to Your servant an understanding heart to judge Your people, that I may discern between good and evil. For who is able to judge this great people of Yours?" The speech pleased the Lord, that Solomon had asked this thing. Then God said to him: "Because you have asked this thing, and have not asked long life for yourself, nor have asked riches for yourself, nor have asked the life of your enemies, but have asked for yourself understanding to discern justice, behold, I have done according to your words; see, I have given you a wise and understanding heart, so that there has not been anyone like you before you, nor shall any like you arise after you. And I have also given you what you have not asked: both riches and honour, so that there shall not be anyone like you among the kings all your days.' 1 Kings 3:6-13 (NKJV)

Elisha...

Then, there is the story of Elisha and the widow.

'A certain woman of the wives of the sons of the prophets cried out to Elisha, saying, "Your servant my husband is dead, and you

know that your servant feared the Lord. And the creditor is coming to take my two sons to be his slaves." So Elisha said to her, "What shall I do for you? Tell me, what do you have in the house?" And she said, "Your maidservant has nothing in the house but a jar of oil." Then he said, "Go, borrow vessels from everywhere, from all your neighbours—empty vessels; do not gather just a few. And when you have come in, you shall shut the door behind you and your sons; then pour it into all those vessels, and set aside the full ones." So she went from him and shut the door behind her and her sons, who brought the vessels to her; and she poured it out. Now it came to pass, when the vessels were full, that she said to her son, "Bring me another vessel." And he said to her, "There is not another vessel." So the oil ceased. Then she came and told the man of God. And he said, "Go, sell the oil and pay your debt; and you and your sons live on the rest." 2 Kings 4:1-7 (NKJV)

I believe the oil would still be flowing if they kept finding enough jars!

God's pattern...

'Then Moses answered and said, "But suppose they will not believe me or listen to my voice; suppose they say, 'The Lord has not appeared to you.'" So the Lord said to him, "What is that in your hand?" He said, "A rod." And He said, "Cast it on the ground." So he cast it on the ground, and it became a serpent; and Moses fled from it. Then the Lord said to Moses, "Reach out your hand and take it by the tail" (and he reached out his hand and caught it, and it became a rod in his hand), "that they may believe that the Lord God of their fathers, the God of Abraham, the God of Isaac, and the God of Jacob, has appeared to you.' Exodus 4:1-5 (NKJV)

When I read these Scriptures, I see a pattern where the Lord used what they already had to create abundance and supernatural success. So, the message is...

Step 1 'Look and see what you have in your hands right now!'

I am always amazed at how few people look at or cannot see what they already have by way of talent, skill or circumstances that the Lord can use. Most people find it hard to see opportunity. I also notice that Jesus used this principle during His ministry on earth. An example of this occurred with the miracle of the loaves and the fish.

Step 2 'Develop a vision for the opportunity you see!'

'A man's heart plans his way, But the Lord directs his steps.' Proverbs 16:9 (NKJV)

Take time with this and ensure that your vision is aligned with the Word of God. If you are unsure check with your pastor.

Step 3 'Write down your vision!'

'Then the Lord answered me and said: "Write the vision And make it plain on tablets, That he may run who reads it.' Habakkuk 2.2 (NKJV)

Many people are afraid to have vision or a plan in case they fail. When you write down your vision or plan, something happens. You are starting the process of declaration over your life. This builds faith to go forward!

Step 4 'Hear the Lord for your next steps!'

You must go to the quiet place to seek and hear from the Lord as to your next steps. They will never be in a straight line. Sometimes you may seem to be going backwards. Think of the astronauts who landed on the Moon. People assume that some genius plotted a course from Cape Canaveral and landed on a specific spot on the moon. Fact is, the spot selected was 500 square miles and the rocket had to readjust direction on average every 10 minutes.

Even so, the rocket eventually landed just inside the 500 square mile mark set. Our journey with the Lord is like that. What is important is that you land in the zone.

Step 5   'Go forward in faith!'

Peter would never have walked on the water if he did not step out of the boat. God's people would never have taken the promised land if they went by what they saw - giants. It is the same for us today. We must take a step otherwise it is not faith!

'Therefore I say to you, whatever things you ask when you pray, believe that you receive them, and you will have them.' Mark 11.24 (NKJV)

The *having* comes after the *receiving*... That is how faith works!

I heard of a story some time ago which influenced me greatly in setting out the steps I have just outlined. During the time of the gold rush in the United States there was a couple who owned a farm and they were having difficulty making ends meet. When the gold rush started they both became excited and desired to find some gold, so they decided to sell their farm and follow the trail, like all the others. They eventually became exhausted, found nothing and ended up bankrupt. They were devastated.

After a period of time they felt inclined to go back and see what had happened to their farm. When they arrived back, they discovered that their farm was surrounded by heavy security and they were not able to enter the property. When they inquired as to what was going on, they discovered that the second biggest gold reserve had been discovered under their farm. Can you imagine how they felt when they discovered what had happened.

Make sure that you do not miss the blessing that the Lord has already placed in your hand. Take time to consider your next steps before moving.

I am conscious as I write this that many may see these steps as applicable to starting a business. This also applies to taking up employment or even if you feel you are called to full-time ministry. The principle in all of this is that whatever the Lord puts in your hand to do, He is able to use this to bless you and prosper you, and through it ensure that you will have no lack and be blessed. If you fail to see this or understand it you will miss the opportunity to receive the Lord's blessing for your life.

I meet many people who are in employment and who see their job as a means to an end, which creates an attitude of chore, and seeing a job only for the purpose of generating income to meet their needs. While this is one of the outcomes, you should realise that your job is the Lord's provision, and He has you in a job to be a witness, and a blessing to your employer. I have heard numerous testimonies of people who approached their job in this way and received amazing favour from their employers.

I also meet many people who seem to have a disconnect between going to work and going to church. This causes them to ask a lot of questions as to how to behave in work, wondering how far they can go in their business before they sin. Such questions highlight to me the disconnect. Whether you are at work, in church or at play there should be no difference in your walk with the Lord. He is your Lord wherever you are and whatever you are doing.

There is no part of your life that the Lord is not interested in and in fact He wants to be in fellowship with you to lead you and guide you in all that you do. If you are conscious of this, you will be amazed how it will change your daily living. I have learned to enjoy the working of this truth in my life for many years and I encourage you to walk with the Lord in this manner from now on. It will change your life!

Finding wealth...

The Bible tells us that if we seek we shall find. This requires diligent focus. You may immediately think that you must start a crusade of activity seeking for the opportunity. However, the Bible tells us that; *'In quietness and trust is your strength.'* (Isaiah 30:15) It also tells us that in that quiet place the Lord will speak; *'Your ears shall hear a word behind you, saying, "This is the way, walk in it," Whenever you turn to the right hand or the left.'* (Isaiah 30:21) This is where you will find your wealth.

During my time of unemployment, I learned many lessons about this. At that time, I was young and fit and while I felt that I might find it difficult to find employment in my field of training, I considered that there were manual jobs that I could do and set out in daily pursuit of one of these without success. I felt so rejected when I went on building sites looking for work and once when I approached the site supervisor asking for work, he asked me to show him my hands and seeing that they were not used to heavy manual work with shovels and such, he advised me that I would not last a week in any job he might have.

Out of this sense of rejection I used to sit at home talking to the Lord whom I was still getting to know, as a little baby getting to know his parents. I would cry out to Him in despair. This started me on a journey to understand what He meant to be in quietness before Him and hear His voice behind my ear telling me to turn to the right or the left. He led me through this time on pathways that made no sense in the natural. I was on a spiritual journey.

This experience has trained me so well in my walk with Him. I encourage you to get into that relationship with Him now and see where He will lead you. You will find the desires of your heart and the fullness of His plan for your life.

I also learned another lesson through this. You see I was a baby Christian during that time. I was like a little chick in a nest with my beak open waiting for my Father to bring me food. He did and

I was never hungry, just like the Lord fed his people in the desert with manna and quail and water so that they were never hungry.

The harvest is always within the seed! If the seed is not planted, the harvest cannot produce.

During this early journey with the Lord, many opportunities came before me to earn income which met urgent provision needs at the time. When this happened, I immediately used to assume that this was now God's plan for my future only to find out after a while that the opportunity stopped. I used to wonder what was happening.

The final episode of this was when somebody asked me to do some sales work for them selling roller shutter doors. They rented a serviced office where I could base myself. I was very successful at this and believed that eventually this is what the Lord had planned for my future provision. One day I came back from lunch to the service office to be told by the receptionist that there were men with guns in my office and not to go in there.

I eventually went to the office and opened the door to find two men with guns pointed towards me. They instructed me to sit on a chair. They then produced their badges and I realised then that they were police detectives. I asked what this was all about but they would not tell me. They asked me who I was working for and what was I working on for them? I told them everything and this put them at ease. They showed me a photo and asked me, "Do you know this person?" I responded, "Yes!" They then told me that I was being used by these people as part of a money laundering racket. They instructed me to pack my case and get out of this job as quickly as I could. Needless to say, I obeyed.

As I drove back to my home in shock and distress knowing that this once again was the end of my source of income. I was crying out to the Lord in the car asking Him what was He doing to me? Before I got home He had shown me very clearly that I must not put my trust in any job, source of income or career, but only trust in Him as my Jehovah Jireh.

I could see how I was beginning to focus my attention on these income sources rather than on Him. Since learning those lessons, my attitude is to depend only on Him whether I have much or little. I have found freedom in this.

This requires us to hear Him, be obedient to what He tells us to do through faith in Him. If we do not take the step of faith, we cannot see the outcome. Peter would never have walked on water if he hadn't of stepped out of the boat onto the water. Most of us become scared of this as sometimes it takes us outside of the boundaries of our natural senses and we do not feel in control. If Jesus is your Lord, then He is in control and not you – trust Him for He Himself said, *'I will never leave you or forsake you.'* Hebrews 13:5

Seeking wealth is self-centred, but to seek *kingdom wealth,* now that's a whole new realm of understanding.

I believe kingdom wealth has the world's wealth incorporated into it. It is much greater than the world's wealth as the world's wealth is a material wealth, but kingdom wealth includes both the spiritual and material wealth. I believe this is the fullness of the inheritance we have in Christ Jesus. If it is given to us as an inheritance, then we must claim it in Jesus' name. If you received an inheritance from your family, you would have to take steps to receive it. It is no different with our kingdom inheritance.

CHAPTER EIGHT

The purpose of wealth...

I believe that the Lord is telling us here that our wealth has two purposes;

- Our sufficiency and abundance in all material things.
- Supporting kingdom ministry.

The Lord promises in this Scripture that He makes all grace, for example, favour and power abound toward us so that you have all sufficiency and abundance to meet your material needs and to support the ministry of your church.

I have come to know that most Christians do not understand this. I have been building up through the earlier chapters of this book to this point which I believe is at the root of why so many Christians and so many churches are in financial starvation and debt today. I have shared how the wealth of the earth fell into enemy hands, how we have the power to take it back in Jesus' Name and how we have this wealth as an inheritance in Jesus' Name. We now see its purpose in our lives according to Scripture.

It is my experience that many Christians do not understand the fullness of the purpose of wealth in their lives. If they did, their lives would be transformed and with it the financial circumstances of church would also be transformed.

The Bible tells us that man's ways are not God's ways for as high as the heavens are above the earth so are God's ways above man's ways. (Isaiah 55:8-9) We must apply Godly wisdom to our wealth and finances.

There is a huge difference between the world's economy and God's economy;

- Man's economy is about *buying and selling*.
- God's economy is about *giving and receiving*.
- Man's economy is all about *the price*.
- God's economy does not count *the cost*.
- Man's economy is *finite*.
- God's economy is *infinite*.

I have shared these many times in business and church workshops and I am always challenged by attendees as to the wisdom of this. I always tell them that if they understood and applied what I was saying, their lives, businesses, ministries, would be transformed.

Purpose Principles

1. Your wealth is not your own. It is the Lord's given to you to use to bless you and to use for His kingdom purpose.

    I will develop this further in the next chapter on stewardship.

2. We should honour the Lord with the first fruits of His wealth provision. It is our acknowledgement of His Lordship, His provision and expresses our gratitude for that which we have received.

> *'Honor the Lord with your possessions, and with the firstfruits of all your increase; So your barns will be filled with plenty, and your vats will overflow with new wine.'* Proverbs 3:9-10 (NKJV)

Most Christians take what is given to them and forget to acknowledge the One who gave it to them. In our daily lives if we give somebody a present, we like to hear the recipient thank us and would be disappointed when this does not happen. How do you think the Lord might feel when we take all He has given and not show gratitude?

We can never express fully our gratitude for what He has done for us, as it is so great. Notice from the Scripture that there is a substantial promise to those who acknowledge Him with our first fruits.

There is a spiritual law of sowing and reaping that applies to the wealth the Lord gives to us.

Recognising this principle and applying it will cause His provision to us to flow freely in our lives. A farmer will never have a harvest unless he sows the seed. If he wishes to have a harvest of wheat, he must first sow wheat seed. He will never have a wheat harvest by sowing barley seed. The seed produces its own kind. The same principle applies to money. I will develop this further in the chapter of giving and receiving.

We all know how important money and wealth are in our personal lives. We must also learn to understand how important they are in the life of the church. The church depends on our financial support to survive, grow and fulfil its mandate. Most churches that I engage with are barely able to survive and do not have the resources to undertake outreach, or support communities where it is based. I believe this is because we who make up the church do not understand this and we become so focused on surviving in our own financial circumstances that we lose sight of the need of the church. This is particularly true when we have debt in our lives or when we are not flowing in the fullness of the Lord's provision.

If we will put God first in this, you will find that He is well able to look after us as we do so. I have experienced for many years as I have engaged in outreach work around the country, new things happening in my business, such as new clients contacting the office wishing to meet me or increases in current business. I firmly believe this is because I put Him first in my daily life.

CHAPTER NINE

Stewardship...

If Jesus is truly Lord of your life, then it is He and not you that is your provider. If He owns it all then our role is that of a steward. A steward is somebody who manages, protects and grows all that is given to him by the owner to manage. Like in the Bible, the owner will check up to see how we've have done with managing what has been given to us. We therefore, need to develop a stewardship mentality. Most of us do not differentiate between **'providership'** and **'stewardship.'** This can cause us a lot of difficulties in our life.

In the early years of starting my business, the Lord taught me a lot of lessons on this. He is still teaching me but the lessons are more advanced. Some of the lessons He taught me were very painful at the time but were all worthwhile and gave me a greater understanding of my walk with Him and the relationship He wants to have with me.

Our Lord is a jealous Lord and if we invite Him to be Lord of our life, He takes this very seriously and is not impressed when we start taking back control through our actions. If we do so, He will never push us aside but instead will allow us to go on and of course we will always end up with a *man outcome* rather than a *God outcome*. When we realise this, we come to repentance and He takes charge again and rescues us. This is a pattern I have come to know very well in my life.

Each wrong choice we make usually has consequences and although the Lord will always rescue us when we realise our mistake and genuinely repent, otherwise, often we continue to have to pay the price for our mistake. This can cause unnecessary pain in our life for a period.

Take for example, a father gives a present of a bicycle to his child with an instruction that he is not to go on the bicycle on his own until he trains him how to ride it. The child, however, decides to go out on the bicycle one day while the father is at work. He cycles out on the road outside the house and crashes into a car that is parked on the road. He falls off, breaks his arm and wrecks the bicycle. Despite his broken arm he gathers up the bicycle whose wheels are now buckled and drags himself and the bicycle back inside the front gate of his house just as his father is turning his car into the driveway coming home from work. The child is now in tears from both the pain of his arm and the embarrassment of his disobedience.

The father sees his child's plight and realises what has happened. The son cries with remorse and asks his father to forgive him. The father puts his arms around him, tells him he is forgiven and then proceeds to take him to the local hospital for an x-ray. The father eventually brings the child home with his arm in plaster. The result of all of this episode is that the child is taught a painful lesson on obedience but has to put up with the consequences of a broken arm for a period and has lost the present of the bicycle that his father gave him.

I am sure we can all recall similar circumstances in our lives. It is the same in our daily walk with our Lord when we are disobedient. Our disobedience usually occurs when we start acting as a provider rather than a steward. It is essential that we develop a high awareness of our relationship with the Lord and our role in the relationship.

When the Lord brought me out of my wilderness and back into the workplace, as shared earlier, I got a job selling life insurance and pensions as an agent paid on a commission-only basis. I knew nothing whatsoever about this business and indeed regarded it as the bottom of the barrel as a career. Nevertheless, in obedience, I accepted the job offer in faith as this was all the Lord put in front of me to do. I had no idea at that time that through this He was bringing me into a completely new world where He would bless me and prosper me, and through it, give me an insight to the world of finance and money, such that I am now prompted by Him to write this book.

I approached this new opportunity with full enthusiasm, learning and studying as quickly as I could. I discovered at an early stage that only one out of 25 people who take up this job last over 12 months. If I had chosen to believe this, I surely would have been discouraged and failed. But this was what my Lord gave me to do and I chose to trust Him to provide and bless me as I progressed.

As I often say; "Those who know WHY will always outperform those who know HOW!"

The business itself that I had come to work in was totally based on sales and product knowledge. It has often been described as; 'selling an intangible asset to somebody who does not see the need.'

I was always a good salesman and as a person was always what some people would call 'driven.'

I found that these skills while helpful did not bring me success. The more I tried to sell, the more I failed and became frustrated. Through this I learned to trust the Lord to be my provider. This meant that I had to learn to wait upon the Lord. As I did, He opened up circumstances that resulted in sales, He prompted me to go in certain directions and brought people across my path. He gave me a vision of a new way for me to develop the business He had given me. This is the vision I work with today in my business. However, He directs my steps. Today, if I try and go ahead of His prompting and direction on my next steps, I always fail. This is the first lesson on stewardship.

'The steps of a good man are ordered by the LORD, And He delights in his way.' Psalm 37:23 (NKJV)

'*A man's heart plans his way, But the Lord directs his steps.*' Proverbs 16:9 (NKJV)

'*He also brought me up out of a horrible pit, Out of the miry clay, And set my feet upon a rock, And established my steps.*' Psalm 40:2 (NKJV)

Lessons on stewardship...

1. **Realise that the Lord is your provider and you are the steward. He is Jehovah Jireh.**

I have come to realise that this requires a change of mindset.

'*And do not be conformed to this world, but be transformed by the renewing of your mind, that you may prove what is that good and acceptable and perfect will of God.*' Romans 12:2 (NKJV)

I find that the biggest challenge in this is striving in contrast to waiting on the Lord. When we start striving we start to act in our own strength again. This never bears fruit and we end up burning out and becoming exhausted. Scripture speaks very clearly to us on this.

'*This is what the Sovereign Lord, the Holy One of Israel, says: "In repentance and rest is your salvation, in quietness and trust is your strength, but you would have none of it. You said, 'No, we will flee on horses.' Therefore you will flee! You said, 'We will ride off on swift horses.' Therefore your pursuers will be swift! A thousand will flee at the threat of one; at the threat of five you will all flee away, till you are left like a flagstaff on a mountain top, like a banner on a hill. Yet the Lord longs to be gracious to you; therefore he will rise up to show you compassion. For the Lord is a God of justice. Blessed are all who wait for him! People of Zion, who live in Jerusalem, you will weep no more. How gracious he will be when you cry for help! As soon as he hears, he will answer you. Although the Lord gives you the bread of adversity and the water of affliction, your teachers will be hidden no more; with your own eyes you will see them. Whether you turn to the right or to the left, your ears will hear a voice behind you, saying, This is the way; walk in it.'* Isaiah 30:15-17

2. Understand your role and relationship with the Lord as a steward.

Obedience is the key to good stewardship. Recognise and understand your responsibility.

- Protect and add value to the assets placed in your charge by the Lord.

- Serve the owner and be accountable to him for the trust the Lord has placed in us.

- Be obedient to His instructions on how the Lord wishes us to manage that which we have been given by Him.

This applies whether you are employed or are in business.

3. Be an active steward as opposed to being passive.

We must approach our stewardship with a proactive attitude responding to the instructions of our Jehovah Jireh. The Lord is not pleased when we have a passive or fearful attitude towards that which He has given us.

Remember how He responded to the steward who hid the talents God gave him because he was afraid of his master. The Lord rebuked him and took the talents he had given him and gave them to the one who had managed to increase the talents he had given him. Our charge is to multiply and replenish what He has given us.

This requires an attitude of mind which takes time to develop and is part of the renewing of our mind that the Scriptures tells us is part of our transformation.

4. Do not put what God has given you into the enemy's hands to manage.

We must keep control of what the Lord gives us. If we fail to do so, the enemy will try and rob it from you. The Lord taught me a very painful lesson some years ago, just because it is *good idea*, does not make it a *God idea*.

My business was growing rapidly and I saw a chance to help those around me, but I never asked God who should sit at the business table He had prepared for me. In my eagerness to improve people's lives I gave them positions and placed them in responsibilities that in many ways, allowed them to manage the business without me being heavily involved.

Two years later I received a notice from Revenue that I owed them a very large sum of money, far greater than my business could afford. This was an amount that the business would have no way of being able to pay. I could not understand how this arose and was in total shock. I discovered that our business had been filing incorrect VAT and PAYE returns for over two years and eventually it all caught up with us. The reason I am using 'us' here is, even though I knew nothing about what had happened, I had offset my stewardship of the business to others. Therefore, I had to accept responsibility.

A week after receiving this Revenue notice, I was called to a meeting by my biggest client who is a plc. At the meeting I was advised that they were cancelling my contract as they had become aware that I had an unsustainable revenue debt. This business provided over fifty percent of my turnover and kept five people in jobs.

While all this was going on, I spent a lot of time in my 'quiet place' in prayer and listening to what the Lord was saying to me. I had placed my trust in others. Ultimately, the buck stops with me before the Lord and indeed before Revenue to whom I owed such a large amount of money.

I repented before the Lord, of decision making without Him, and I knew that He would rescue me from my mistakes if my motives were pure.

'If you say, "The Lord is my refuge," and you make the Most High your dwelling, no harm will overtake you, no disaster will come near your tent. For he will command his angels concerning you to guard you in all your ways; they will lift you up in their hands, so that you will not strike your foot against a stone.' Psalm 91:9-12

I kept declaring this Scripture to myself aloud during this time. The strength, courage and trust this gave me was amazing even though the circumstances looked impossible.

At the end of my meeting with my biggest client, the manager acknowledged to me that he was saddened to have to give me such bad news and suggested that it might be possible to get one of the other providers to give me *a few bob* for the contract. He asked if I would like him to find out. I was barely listening to him as I was in shock. I told him to go ahead.

 **Don't expect an increase, until you possess what you have.**

One month after this meeting I signed a deal with another provider to sell him the contract for three-times the size of my Revenue debt. This deal, gave me the money to clear the debt in full. We need to remember: Repentance in God will turn your situation around. We serve an amazing and supernatural God whose promises can never fail to be fulfilled in the lives of those who will choose to believe them. I chose to do so on this and declared it daily into my life not knowing how it might be possible. I didn't need to know. I needed to trust Him to know.

Today this is long since behind me. However, the lessons I learned through this will always remain with me. I had to make immediate changes to my business on learning this lesson. The biggest part of this was to ensure that the control of the business finances was brought back into my control and under the supervision of me. Like in as I shared earlier, what is in your hand? I also brought my wife Mary into the business to take charge of all the bookkeeping and my children are in the business now too.

Out of this experience, I have also witnessed the Lord's anointing surge in the life of my daughter Julie who took control of the day-to-day management of the business. The daughter who sat on my knee when young, now has the responsibility of a business sitting on her knee and she's anointed to run it. The Lord knew better and what a joy it is for all of my family.

Stewardship of money...

Money is meant to be your servant, not a master that rules over you. Jesus said that money is the least area in trusting God.

'So if you have not been trustworthy in handling worldly wealth, who will trust you with true riches? And if you have not been trustworthy with someone else's property, who will give you property of your own?' Luke 16:11-12

So how should we start to become a steward of our money and become trustworthy in what is the least in God's eyes?

STEWARDSHIP

1. Undertake a Financial Health Check of your finances.

Financial Health Check

Name:

Assets	Type	€	Liabilities	Type	€	Improvements	Notes
1			1				
2			2				
3			3				
4			4				
5			5				
6			6				
Total					Total		
Liabilities							
Surplus/Deficit							

Income	Type	€/week	Outgoings	Type	€/week		
1			1. Mortgage				
2			2. Loans				
3			3. Credit Cards				
4			4. Hse Insurance				
5			5. Life Insurance				
6			6. Electric				
			7. Telephone				
			8. Gas/Oil				
			9. Motor Petrol				
			Tax				
			Insurance				
			Maintenance				
			10. Groceries				
			11. Kids School				
			12. Kids pocket money				
			13. Entertainment				
			14. Membership/Subs				
			15. Other				
Total			Total				
Outgoings							
Surplus/Deficit							

2. Are you Bleeding?

If you were a doctor and a patient came to you that had been in an accident and was bleeding badly, the first thing you would likely do is to stop the bleeding as this would stabilise the patient. When this is done you would likely then go and diagnose the cause and any other injuries. It is the same with money!

I meet so many people in my life who are not making ends meet. In other words, their outgoings are greater than their income – they are bleeding!

3. Stop the Bleeding.

Make decisions as to how you can balance your income and outgoings. This may mean talking to your mortgage provider, your bank or other lender, and in some cases make decisions to cut back on some unnecessary spending. You cannot go forward until you do this and if you try to go forward, you will only become more frustrated as your bleeding will make you weaker.

4. Restructure and where possible settle your debts.

Short-term debt and particularly credit card debt can cause huge cash flow problems and, in some cases, can be never ending due to high interest rates. Settlement or restructuring of these debts can have huge benefits. When you fail to pay your credit card on time the bank or credit card company usually starts making a fortune as it compounds the interest which is so high that you never get to pay down the capital. They write to you and tell you are in default while all the time they are feasting on the interest you are charged.

5. **Examine any areas of your finances where satan may be robbing you and put an end to it in Jesus' Name.**

Did you ever have a wage increase or a great week of income only to find that as soon as it happened a bill came in that took it all away? This was my experience for far too many years until I realised what was happening. Once I did, I immediately took authority over the situation and put an end to this happening. Much of the problem was caused by myself not organising my income and outgoing properly. Doors were left open in my finances which allowed satan to come in and use my circumstances to attack me.

6. **Start seeking out God's plan for your life.**

If you have gone through the first four steps you will find that you have freedom to take time in the *quiet place* with the Lord to hear His plans for your future. You can be confident that His only desire is that you prosper in **all** areas of your life.

*'And God is able to make
all grace abound toward you, that you,
always having all sufficiency in all things,
may have an abundance
for every good work.'*

2 Corinthians 9:8 (NKJV)

CHAPTER TEN

Giving and receiving...

We have explored many areas of Scripture relating to wealth, money and its purpose. We have seen that it is the Lord's desire and plan that we have and enjoy wealth in our lives. Let us again look at one of the key Scriptures relating to the purpose of wealth in our lives.

'And God is able to make all grace abound toward you, so that you, always having all sufficiency in all things, may have an abundance for every good work.' 2 Corinthians 9:8 (NKJV)

I believe that all blessings we receive have two purposes.

1. Our own benefit, provision and edification.
2. To share with others.

The principle of sharing has huge significance in kingdom living. We see from the earlier chapters that our wealth is not our own. We are but stewards of the wealth the Lord gives us. The wealth is for our blessing and His work. He has asked us to acknowledge Him with the first fruits of His provision. I believe there is a spiritual law at work in all of this. It is the law of sowing and reaping. Throughout the Bible we find this law at work.

- The widow and her last loaf of bread.
- The widow and the jar of oil.
- The loaves and the fishes.

The business of farming is totally based on sowing and reaping. If the farmer does not sow seed he cannot expect a crop. If the farmer does not sow the seed for a particular crop, all kinds of grass will grow on his lands, some good, some bad. Weeds and all kinds of unwanted plants will also grow up on the land. It will be of no benefit to the farmer and only give him problems. I believe it is the same with our spiritual life.

Most people reading this will assume I am talking about money. What about sowing love, our time, our energy, our attitude, or our encouragement? When we sow our time, energy, encouragement or money into the lives of others, we always bless them and we are blessed ourselves in doing so. I find that as we practice sowing, we develop a sowing mentality. I believe this is a key to opening up a blessed life.

'And just as you want men to do to you, you also do to them likewise.' Luke 6:31 (NKJV)

When I share these principles in meetings, I am sometimes challenged by the people in attendance, as they feel that if you want to be successful you must put yourself and your business first and sometimes you have to step on people's toes to succeed. I always respond by telling them that if they apply the principles I share they would be much more successful.

'For My thoughts are not your thoughts, Nor are your ways My ways," says the Lord. "For as the heavens are higher than the earth, So are My ways higher than your ways, And My thoughts than your thoughts.' Isaiah 55:8-9 (NKJV)

Within a church environment, the subject of giving and receiving is much spoken of in the context of tithing. Many ministries apply a lot of pressure on congregations to tithe and give to their ministries.

There is no doubt that the Scriptures make it clear that tithing and giving should be part of our daily walk with the Lord. It also seems clear to me that we should tithe and give, not because we have to, but because we want to.

'Give generously to them and do so without a grudging heart; then because of this the Lord your God will bless you in all your work and in everything you put your hand to.' Deuteronomy 15:10

'If it is to encourage, then give encouragement; if it is giving, then give generously; if it is to lead, do it diligently; if it is to show mercy, do it cheerfully.' Romans 12:8

The principle of giving of our first fruits and tithing to the Lord are very clearly set out in Scripture. Some say that the requirement to tithe was an Old Testament practice. This is not true as the practice of tithing is also set out in the New Testament and is one of the practices carried over from the Old to the New Testament. I believe this is because there is a spiritual principle and law at work in our tithing. It is the one aspect of God's Word where He challenges us to test Him in this.

'Will a man rob God? Yet you have robbed Me! But you say, 'In what way have we robbed You?' In tithes and offerings. You are cursed with a curse, For you have robbed Me, Even this whole nation. Bring all the tithes into the storehouse, That there may be food in My house, And try Me now in this," Says the Lord of hosts, "If I will not open for you the windows of heaven And pour out for you such blessing That there will not be room enough to receive it.'
Malachi 3:8-10

This Scripture is spoken of almost at all times when the subject of giving is preached. There is always a danger that those who hear it are challenged by it and miss the incredible blessing and promise contained in the Scripture. Giving because *you have to* brings no blessings. Giving because *you want to* always brings blessings. Can you say that out loud... Giving because *you have to* brings no blessings! Giving because *you want to* always brings blessings!

'God is not a man, that He should lie, Nor a son of man, that He should repent. Has He said, and will He not do? Or has He spoken, and will He not make it good? Behold, I have received a command to bless; He has blessed, and I cannot reverse it.' Numbers 23:19-20 (NKJV)

There is another Scripture that is regularly used when preaching on giving. It carries again an incredible promise. Not only does this Scripture clearly set out the promise but it also provides an insight on how the promise will be fulfilled and also puts in context much of what I have already gone through in the earlier chapters of this book.

'Give, and it shall be given unto you; good measure, pressed down, and shaken together, and running over, shall men give into your bosom. For with the same measure that ye mete withal it shall be measured to you again.' Luke 6:38 (KJV)

The words *'shall men give into your bosom'* gives us insight and understanding of how you will receive the blessing. First of all, we do not have to do anything to receive it as the promise is that it will be given into your bosom. The second aspect of this and I believe it specifically relates to money and wealth is set out in another Scripture and relates to wealth transfer.

'A good man leaves an inheritance to his children's children, But the wealth of the sinner is stored up for the righteous.' Proverbs 13:22 (NKJV)

'And the Lord had given the people favour in the sight of the Egyptians, so that they granted them what they requested. Thus they plundered the Egyptians.' Exodus 12:36 (NKJV)

Remember in the earlier chapters I showed how satan continues to have control of the world's wealth until Jesus returns. However, those of us who are God's children have been restored to have dominion over the earth through what Jesus did for us. We must exercise faith and take it back, not just for ourselves but for the church and its ministry here on earth until Jesus returns.

Sowing a seed...

Many of God's children today have a desire and a heart to give generously but often complain that they have no seed to sow. This is particularly true with people who are trying to deal with debt or unemployment. If the widow who was about to cook her last piece of bread for her child and herself did not give it instead to Elijah she would never have seen the Lord's blessing. Most people either do not realise or forget the promise of God relating to seed.

'Now may He who supplies seed to the sower, and bread for food, supply and multiply the seed you have sown and increase the fruits of your righteousness.' 2 Corinthians 9:10 (NKJV)

The Lord provides us with the seed to sow. If this is so, then we should always be able to tithe and give, no matter what our circumstances. Debt and lack of income become excuses in these circumstances. The question is, are you eating the seed the Lord has given you to sow? If this is so, how then can you ever reap as without a seed sown, there can be no crop!

We must have a steward's mentality when it comes to giving and understand there is a spiritual law underpinning this. If we sow we will reap. Ask any farmer and he will confirm this. The farmer will always be conscious of setting aside seed from his crop so that he has seed for his next crop. I have yet to meet a Christian who gives generously who has not had their needs met.

Sowing is best done when you know the purpose and have expectation of reaping. This is faith in action. Many of us are afraid to take the step to give as we feel we cannot afford to. I say you cannot afford **not to** as the spiritual blessings that is yours when you give will be missed and your prosperity will be diminished.

I had great difficulty in the beginning with giving as I was in such a bad place financially. The story of the widow and her last loaf of bread used to bother me as I did not seem to have her faith. I was often challenged by satan on this who tried many times to bring me into condemnation.

I always held my ground on this as I knew that; *'there is now no condemnation for those who are in Christ Jesus.'* (Romans 8:1) Over time the Lord encouraged me to give and gradually I saw the blessing that resulted from my step of faith. This increased my faith for the next step until I reached the place I am in today where I no longer try to hold on to that which is not mine but His. In doing so, I have come to know and experience the flow of finance into and through my life for my abundant provision and for the work of His kingdom.

If God can get money through you, He will get money to you!

CHAPTER ELEVEN

Praying for finances...

Throughout the Bible we are continually reminded of the role of prayer in the life of a Christian. It is the point of interaction between God and man. The biggest challenge we face with prayer is;

- How to pray effectively.
- Faith to receive answered prayer.

The Lord has taught me so much about effective prayer and praying in faith over the many years walking under His Lordship. I want to share my experiences on this with you in this chapter and in doing so, provide Scriptural reference to what I have learned.

When I first surrendered to the Lordship of Jesus, I did not know Him. I just knew *about* Him. There is a huge difference in knowing somebody personally, then knowing *everything* about somebody. Because of this I did not know how to pray to Him. When I look back, I would describe my so-called prayer interaction with Him as just talking to Him about my circumstances and my needs. I told Him also a lot about how I was feeling. I often cried out to Him and regularly complained to Him. I am sure many of you reading this will identify with what I am sharing.

One of the parts of Scripture that captured me early in my walk was the meaning of 'Eternal Life.'

'And this is eternal life, that they may know You, the only true God, and Jesus Christ whom You have sent.' John 17:3 (NKJV)

In the original Greek text, the word 'Ginosko' is used. This means to know intimately or to have a personal intimate relationship. Therefore, it is God's desire that we would have a personal intimate relationship with Him. I longed to experience this type of relationship with Him. I know we will never experience the fullness of this relationship until we go and be with Him in heaven. However, my desire was and always will be to have as intimate a relationship with Him as possible while I remain in the flesh here on earth.

The image of a Father's attitude towards His children that is portrayed many times in Scripture also helped me greatly as a reference point in understanding the type of relationship He wishes to have with me.

'Or what man is there among you who, if his son asks for bread, will give him a stone? Or if he asks for a fish, will he give him a serpent?' Matthew 7:9-10 (NKJV)

'Therefore I say to you, do not worry about your life, what you will eat or what you will drink; nor about your body, what you will put on. Is not life more than food and the body more than clothing? Look at the birds of the air, for they neither sow nor reap nor gather into barns; yet your heavenly Father feeds them. Are you not of more value than they? Which of you by worrying can add one cubit to his stature? "So why do you worry about clothing? Consider the lilies of the field, how they grow: they neither toil nor spin; and yet I say to you that even Solomon in all his glory was not arrayed like one of these. Now if God so clothes the grass of the field, which today is, and tomorrow is thrown into the oven, will He not much more clothe you, O you of little faith?' Matthew 6:25-30 (NKJV)

These Scriptures helped me so much in my early years walking with him. I had three young children at that time that I was unable to provide for. We had a roof over their heads that I knew I could not keep. I used to reflect on how I felt towards them in this situation and I felt the overwhelming desire that I had to ensure that they would be okay. I used to say to the Lord how I would willingly give up my life that they would have theirs. This feeling would give me some insight into how my Lord felt about me and my family.

'And in that day you will ask Me nothing. Most assuredly, I say to you, whatever you ask the Father in My name He will give you. Until now you have asked nothing in My name. Ask, and you will receive, that your joy may be full.' John 16:23-24 (NKJV)

I came to understand during these early years also, that the end of us, is the beginning of Him. It is through His Holy Spirit that we grow in relationship with Him. All He wants from us as we grow in Him, is our availability and our trust and faith in Him. Even our faith in Him is not of ourselves, as it is a gift that the Lord gives us. Our ability has nothing to do with this.

I have also come to understand that at the beginning of our relationship with Him, He tends to our needs just like a mother tends to her new baby. As the child grows, the mother teaches her baby until they are able to do things themselves such as walking.

I am also reminded of the story of the eagle. The eagle makes her nest in the high cliffs and when the chicks are born, she goes and gathers food for them and places it in the chick's mouths to feed. Eventually as the chicks grow and get stronger, a time comes when the mother decides it is time for the chicks to leave the nest. She pushes the chicks out of the nest, high up on the cliff. This is the only way the chicks will learn to fly.

I believe the Lord brings us to a place in our relationship with Him where He throws us out of the nest so that we can learn to be in Him who He says we are. Are you still hanging on to the nest and afraid to trust Him for all He has promised you? You do not need much faith when the Lord is placing the food in your mouth!

I have experienced this transition in my relationship with Him. It has also changed my prayer life. I meet many Christians who have difficulty in dealing with this change. If this is you, then I pray that through what I share with you on this, you will find the fullness of how the Lord wants to engage with you.

'For though by this time you ought to be teachers, you need someone to teach you again the first principles of the oracles of God; and you have come to need milk and not solid food. "For everyone who partakes only of milk is unskilled in the word of righteousness, for he is a babe.' Hebrews 5:12-13 (NKJV)

I realise that these words may be really challenging to you. Let me ask you a question... Do you experience answered prayer on a daily basis? I believe you should. Could the reason be something to do with the possibility that the Lord is trying to teach you to grow in Him and change from being a little chick to being a mature *joint heir* with Him in this kingdom we live in while on earth.

'And if children, then heirs—heirs of God and joint heirs with Christ, if indeed we suffer with Him, that we may also be glorified together.' Romans 8:17 (NKJV)

So how should we pray to have effective outcomes? Jesus gives us clear instruction on this and is as follows;

'And when you pray, you shall not be like the hypocrites. For they love to pray standing in the synagogues and on the corners of the streets, that they may be seen by men. Assuredly, I say to you, they have their reward. But you, when you pray, go into your room, and when you have shut your door, pray to your Father who is in the secret place; and your Father who sees in secret will reward you openly. And when you pray, do not use vain repetitions as the heathen do. For they think that they will be heard for their many words. Therefore do not be like them. For your Father knows the things you have need of before you ask Him.' Matthew 6:5-8 (NKJV)

This teaching of Jesus should cause us to review and reflect on how we pray. For example, when we think we are praying, are we really praying or complaining? I believe that the Lord is compassionate towards us in our needs. However, while this is so, it is faith that moves God.

Throughout the Bible, answered prayer is always based on faith. Remember the woman with the issue of blood. It was because of her faith that she was healed.

We need to ask ourselves when we pray whether we are praying in hope or praying in faith. There is a big difference. So how do we differentiate as to whether we pray in hope or in faith. Let us look at what faith means;

'Now faith is the substance of things hoped for, the evidence of things not seen.' Hebrews 11:1 (NKJV)

We can see from this Scripture that faith is a higher level of confidence that the Lord will answer and give us what we hope for. How can we have this substance? Firstly, we must remember that it is not man-made, because it is a gift from God. So how do we acquire this gift?

'So then faith comes by hearing, and hearing by the word of God.' Romans 10:17 (NKJV)

It is clear from this that if we want to grow our faith, we must be a reader of the Word of God. There is a spiritual power in the Word that builds us up in faith to receive answers to our prayer.

As I outlined earlier, I certainly acted as a little chick in a nest waiting on the Lord to feed me. As I grew, I came to realise that faith without works is dead. This meant that I had to take steps in faith to trust and believe God to answer my prayer.

He was now teaching me to understand the power and authority in Jesus' Name that He had placed within me. This took time to develop and is still a work in progress. The woman with the issue of blood (Luke 8:43-48) would not be healed if she did not push through the crowd and touch the hem of Jesus' garment.

There are two Scriptures which provide two promises that Jesus gave us to ensure answered prayer. The first of these promises was spoken by Jesus when the apostles saw that the fig tree that Jesus had cursed the previous day had withered to the ground as they passed by the next day.

'So Jesus answered and said to them, "Assuredly, I say to you, if you have faith and do not doubt, you will not only do what was done to the fig tree, but also if you say to this mountain, 'Be removed and be cast into the sea,' it will be done. And whatever things you ask in prayer, believing, you will receive.' Matthew 21:21-22 (NKJV)

This is an amazing promise. It tells us that we can have whatever we say! It also says the promise is for 'whosoever.' That means you and me!

The conditions for fulfilment are 'say' and 'believe.'

I believe there is a huge significance to our saying as it is speaking out loud, declaring. It also starts the process of believing which is faith. Scripture tells us that *'faith comes by hearing and hearing by the Word of God.'* (Romans 10:17) When we speak out we hear and when we hear ourselves speak or declare, I believe it effects our heart and spirit. Are we having what we declare or declaring what we have?

Remember that God created the world and all things in it by speaking and declaring it into being. Believing must always come before seeing, otherwise it would not be faith. Most of us start believing when we have seen. You will never receive answers to prayer if you believe only when you see. It is not faith then.

This Scripture has been used widely by those who teach a *'name it and claim it'* message and which has caused a lot of argument within church and has caused a lot of Christians to go down cul de sac's in their walk with the Lord. If our prayer motives are selfish in their nature we cannot expect answers to prayer.

In my experience of answered prayer, I have come to realise that whatever our prayer need is, we should find the promise of God concerning the matter. This ensures that we find His will on the matter and also His promise.

Remember His promises can never fail to be fulfilled in our lives if we will believe. God promised his people a promised land when they left Egypt but most of them did not believe Him and therefore, never received the fulfilment of the promise.

'God is not a man, that he should lie; neither the son of man, that he should repent: hath he said, and shall he not do it? or hath he spoken, and shall he not make it good?' Numbers 23:19 (KJV)

The second promise was also spoken by Jesus. This time it was when He was with His disciples at the last supper just before He was betrayed.

'If you abide in Me, and My words abide in you, you will ask what you desire, and it shall be done for you. By this My Father is glorified, that you bear much fruit; so you will be My disciples.' John 15:7-8 (NKJV)

Here Jesus makes another promise and not only makes a promise but also tells us why He has promised. I believe this also applies to 'whosoever' and also 'whatsoever.'

The conditions here are that you are abiding in Him and also that His words are abiding in you. Your continued surrender to Him and your continued mindfulness of His word fulfil these conditions and based on which, your prayer **will** be answered. We must always consider our motives and His promises when we pray.

CHAPTER 12

Learning about money…

I have outlined a lot of general lessons that I have experienced. I now want to share specific lessons I have learned in my prayer life about money. It is very important to understand the context, role and infrastructure that money plays as we live here on earth. This will help greatly in dealing with both lack and abundance of money in our life. Taking this into account let me now set out the lessons that I have learned to date. Please remember as I share on this, like us all, I am still a work in progress.

- **There is NO money in heaven!**

    Scripture tells us extensively that heaven has streets of gold and is adorned with every precious metal. Money only operates here on earth and is merely a currency that has *perceived* value. If this currency was introduced by God from heaven into the earth it would be regarded as counterfeit. So expecting God to send down money into your life will not happen. This should influence how we pray to the Lord.

- **Money derives from wealth.**

  We must therefore, pray for the power to get wealth which is His promise. We must be attentive to all the Lord is placing in your hands and also learn to hear His voice so that He can give direction.

- **The Lord is the provider!**

  We must trust Him to be our provider and not step in ourselves as a provider which is effectively taking back lordship. In times of lack this becomes a challenge as we can easily start striving.

- **We have dominion and authority with money!**

  This is entirely Scriptural. The challenge is to exercise our authority in Jesus' name. This will only come with practice.

- **We must take back what the enemy has robbed and is robbing from us!**

  This requires exercising our authority in Jesus' Name. This must become a prayer point in our daily lives.

- **We must demand that the enemy releases what he is holding back from us!**

  This again should be our daily prayer point.

- **We must use the money as the Lord has instructed.**

  Remember the principle of sowing and reaping and apply it!

Final thoughts...

If you feel from reading this book that you would like to come into relationship with the Lord of whom I have spoken, all you need to do is to declare this prayer. Scripture informs us in Romans 10:9; *'That if you confess with your mouth the Lord Jesus and believe in your heart that God has raised Him from the dead, you will be saved.'*

Pray this simple prayer and invite Him into your heart...

Lord...

I believe that you are the Creator of this world and all things in it. I confess that I am a sinner and cannot be saved through my own effort. I believe and accept that because of this you sent your only Son, Jesus to pay the price for my sinfulness. I ask you to forgive me for all my sins. I now surrender unto your Lordship and ask you to be Lord of my life from this day on.

Thank you Lord.

Signed...

Date..

If you have made this declaration, you are now saved. Congratulations! I recommend that you find a church where you can grow and receive support and encouragement.

I want you to know that God has a plan for your life. Seek to find it and there you will find prosperity and fulfilment.

The Lord has declared that He knew you before you were formed in your mother's womb and that you are fearfully and wonderfully made.

'The Lord bless you and keep you; The Lord make His face shine upon you, And be gracious to you; The Lord lift up His countenance upon you, And give you peace.' Numbers 6:24-26

Your daily declaration...

I thank You Lord that You knew me before I was formed in my mother's womb. I thank You Lord that I am fearfully and wonderfully made. I thank You Lord that You created me in Your image and likeness and to have fellowship with me. (Genesis 1:26)

I thank You Lord for this day and ask You to be Lord over every step I take, every word I speak and everything I put my hand to. I thank You that because You are my Lord this day, I am like a tree planted by rivers of living waters that brings forth fruit in season, whose leaf shall not wither and whatever I do shall prosper. (Psalm 1:3)

I make You my dwelling place this day and therefore, no harm shall befall me, no accident shall overtake me and no calamity shall come near my home because You send your angels to guard and protect me, to lift me up lest I strike my foot against a stone. (Psalm 91:9-12)

I believe in You Lord and decide to walk by Faith in You. Jesus, You are the author and developer of my faith. My Faith comes by hearing and hearing by your Word. (Romans 10:17)

I let Your Word dwell in me always and trust that You would began a good work in me and will continue to the day of Christ's return. (Philippians 1:6)

I reside in the kingdom of God's dear Son and the law of the Spirit of Life in Christ has set me free from the law of sin and death. I fear not for God has given me a spirit of power of love and a sound mind. I do not fret or have anxiety about anything. I do not have a care for greater is He who is in me than he who is in the world. (Romans 8:2, 2 Timothy 1:7, 1 John 4:4)

No weapon formed against me will prosper. Every tongue that rises against me in judgement shall be shown to be in the wrong for God is on my side and is my defender. (Isaiah 54:17)

My God you supply all my needs according to your riches in glory in Christ. I will not worry about the food I eat or the clothes I wear for you are my Jehovah Jireh. (Philippians 4:19, Matthew 6:25)

I am the body of Christ. I am redeemed from the curse of sin because Jesus bore my sicknesses and diseases on His own body. For by His wounds I am healed. I forbid any sickness or disease to live in my body. Every organ and every tissue of my body functions just as You have created it. (Galatians 3.13, Matthew 8:17)

I have the mind of Christ and bring every thought into captivity and obedience to Christ. My mind is fixed on my Lord Jehovah. I trust in the Lord and I am in perfect peace. (1 Corinthians 2:16, 2 Corinthians 10:5)

I commit and trust wholly on the Lord. He will cause my thoughts to become agreeable to His will and so shall my plans be established and succeed. I am a world overcomer because I am born of God. I am His workmanship recreated in Christ Jesus. My Father God is all the while at work in me to will and do His good pleasure. I can do all things through Christ who strengthens me. (Philippians 2:13)

You are a God of abundance and no lack. Therefore, because You are my Lord I will have abundance and no lack in my house this day. (2 Corinthians 9:8)

I now go forth with praise and thanksgiving, confident that, just as You have promised, whatever I do this day will prosper in Jesus Name.

If you need help or advice
for your business or personal finances,
Liam and his team are only a call away.

To contact the author visit
www.33Plus3.com
E. info@33Plus3.com

Write to
33Plus3
12-13 Whitefiars
Peters Row
Aungier Street
Dublin 2
Ireland

INSPIRED TO WRITE A BOOK?

Contact

Maurice Wylie Media

Inspirational Christian Publisher

Based in Northern Ireland and distributing across the world.

www.MauriceWylieMedia.com

www.ingramcontent.com/pod-product-compliance
Lightning Source LLC
Chambersburg PA
CBHW070115080526
44586CB00013B/1305